PUPPETS

How politicians and the media have manipulated Americans for 100 years and what we must do to correct it and save America.

By Rick Foster

Introduction

You, yes you, have been a puppet all your life. You have been played like a puppet by a very skillful puppeteer. You have been told how to think and consequently how to act. Yes, you have been manipulated. All of us have been manipulated at some time. Not me, you say? No one has their hand up my back. No one is pulling my strings. Read on, and you will see otherwise. You will see who, how, and why you have been manipulated.

Margaret Thatcher once said that Europe was built by history, but America was built on a philosophy. There's a lot of truth to that, but what philosophy? The philosophy used to be very different than it is today. The American experiment, as some have called this philosophy, said the people were in charge instead of the government or one monarch or dictator. School children were taught that America was a special place because of this philosophy. If someone was raised in America in the 50's and 60's and listened, somewhat at least, to their teachers in history class, like most students, they probably took what they were told as gospel. They typically didn't question what the history books said because they were sent to school, after all, to learn from the teachers, and for the most part teachers didn't have a political agenda back then. They were there to teach subjects like reading, writing, and arithmetic (that's math for the younger readers who have never heard of arithmetic) and history. They taught what was written in the textbooks picked by their community. Some of this history was beneficial and accurate, and some, as they say today, had a positive spin put on it. Although there may have been some policies or ideas that not everyone would agree were good for America, for the most part, children in this country were taught mostly positive things about the Presidents and leaders. And consequently, most people grew up with a patriotic feeling about America. Heroes were an important part of the image of America. Heroes such as Audie Murphy, John Wayne, Roy Rogers, Hop-Along Cassidy, Davey Crockett, Jim Thorpe, Jesse Owens, and later Roger Staubach, Clark Gable, Jimmy Stewart, Glen Ford, and John Wayne. Yes, John Wayne was mentioned twice. He is worth mentioning twice. The media didn't go out of their way to show the weaknesses of these patriots, just their strengths, and they had plenty of weaknesses, well, except for Roger Staubach. Young boys grew up wanting to be heroes. They grew up wanting to be strong and wanting to stand up for their country. Fathers were heroes and role models, and their sons were taught how a man was supposed to act. A man was supposed to stand up for people who couldn't stand up for themselves and to protect women and children. Young men were taught manners and to act like a gentleman. What does that mean, gentleman? Women were not pampered because they were weak. Actually just the opposite was true. Women were the anchor for the family. They were to be taken care of and protected, and they also took care of and protected their family. Children were taught to respect their parents and their "elders." They were taught the golden rule. Was this indoctrination a good thing? Look at what is going on in the world today. Whatever feels good do it. Manners are not taught anymore because that might make that child feel insecure or subservient. They're not a child, they're just a small person. When children misbehaved with their parents or at school, until the 90s, they received a good dose of corporal punishment. For the young people who don't understand that term, it means they got a butt-whipping that would usually change their attitude and the bad behavior would usually cease pretty quick. Today, parents or school principals caught spanking children would be on the news and maybe even in jail. As children turned into teenagers, bad behavior might result in getting grounded, or having their car keys taken away would get their attention. Most baby-boomers probably have experienced some of these barbaric practices. Kids were spanked, and grounded, and yelled at, and they survived and became mannerly, respectful adults because of it. By no means perfect adults. They still had their imperfections, but overall they treated each other with more respect than what is seen today. It was a common practice to pray before school and then say the Pledge of Allegiance. Families went to the church of their choice, and even though their neighbor went to a different church, it didn't matter. Americans, no matter what color or ethnicity, were indoctrinated by a society who believed God and Country and family were really what mattered.

America is now changing rapidly. For the first time in almost 100 years, many people around the world, and within, are no longer looking at America as the leader of the free world. Some schools are teaching students that our flag is offensive to some. In some states, the terms father and mother have been removed from public records. Values that were an important part of the history of America have been replaced with whatever is politically correct. Had someone suggested some of these changes 20 years ago, most Americans would have remarked, "That's absurd."

Ronald Reagan's "Shining City on a Hill" has been tarnished somewhat. Why is this happening?

Different dictionaries define the word manipulated in different ways.

They include: To move, arrange, control, influence or manage shrewdly, or to control in a skillful manner. The manipulators are truly skillful. They control people without their knowing they have been controlled.

It's not hard to manipulate someone's thinking apparently. Simply tell some stories, myths, or lies, and then tell some anecdotes repeatedly to support your manipulations, and suddenly those stories somehow become facts in people's minds. A recent article in USA Today stated that the public is more gullible than ever. The article talked about a study that showed the public is easily fooled by bogus news stories. A group of 5,200 people were shown bogus news stories from a made-up USA Today paper inspired by the old movie "Back to the Future." The study showed that most of the people in the study group believed the stories. How could they be so easily manipulated? Manipulations are usually based on myths or lies. Have someone who is influential repeat the lies, put out some emotional stories or anecdotes to support the lies, and the storyteller will not only get a follower but many times an advocate. Sometimes it is done in such a subtle way the readers or listeners don't even know it's happening. As someone gets older, it seems to become easier to be manipulated. Don't think it is that easy to be manipulated? In 1938, Orson Welles a well-known actor, broadcast a series of simulated news bulletins from H.G. Wells novel, "War of the Worlds." Orson's voice and demeanor made the announcements sound so real that many listeners thought Martians were actually invading the earth. Even though there was a disclaimer at the start of the show, police stations received numerous calls from panicked listeners. Later when announcers told people what had happened, some people accused them of covering up the truth. They were convinced that aliens were invading!

The public has been conditioned to believe if something is in writing or broadcast on TV, it must be true. Plenty of evidence sits next to the cashier at the grocery store. There is almost always a large rack of tabloids for customers to look at while they are in line. Almost any day, there are headlines on these tabloids that say some celebrity or politician is really an alien and these tabloids sell millions of copies.

This book will attempt to show in very plain talk how politicians, individuals, large corporations, and the media have manipulated Americans for a long time and how with the help of TV, etc., they are getting better and better at this game as time goes by. This is about how these manipulations have adversely affected the American way of life in many ways. These manipulations affect the US economy, public safety, and especially relationships with each other.

Who are these manipulators? The simple answer is politicians, corporations, and the media, especially groups of media that are tied closely to certain political parties.

In America's history, most of the people becoming elected to Congress or the presidency were usually small business owners who gave up six or eight years of their life to help or give service to their country. Today, however, politicians do all they can to get elected and stay elected, many times for over 30 years. To do this, they have learned how to play the game better than anyone. By the way, approximately 66% of democratic congresspeople were lawyers before they were elected to office. Approximately 20% of Republicans are lawyers. Why would a successful lawyer want to spend the rest of his life in Congress or the Senate if it weren't more profitable than what they were already doing? If someone ever has watched a skillful trial lawyer, it is very evident that they learned how to play the game. And as mentioned before, many politicians were lawyers in their past. In a comedy called "The Best Little Whorehouse in Texas," the Governor was asked questions by the media and after he answered, the media would ask, "what did he say"? It's like they take a class somewhere when they are running for office that teaches them how to not answer a question. Answering a question directly could cost them votes, and votes are what this game is ultimately all about. The game goes something like this, someone asks a politician a tough question, simply deflect it with another issue that people are passionate about. When they don't want to answer a question they just say something like, "I think the question we should be asking is…" Another issue comes up, another deflection. Some people have become masters at this game. And the masters have learned that manipulation uses emotion rather than reason or logic. Pull peoples heart strings, work on their emotions, and reason goes right out the window. Facts mean nothing if people are upset. Once those emotions start flowing any attempt to change someone's mind falls on deaf ears. This manipulation has been going on for a long time.

History

"Those who can make you believe absurdities can make you commit atrocities." Voltaire

Despotic leaders or dictators have always been charismatic and very influential people. Many times these leaders came out of no-where. People wondered how a German Army Corporal could start from nothing and become one of the most powerful, most controlling, and, therefore, diabolic leaders in the history of mankind.

Germany had just lost World War I. They were humiliated and were being punished for waging war against the allies. This economic punishment put Germany into a severe depression. Unemployment soared. Inflation soared. The German people were hungry for some good news. Hitler came along at the right time. He knew ,that his people were upset about losing the war and the resulting economy, and, therefore he focused on promising jobs and giving the people of Germany some respect back after their defeat in WWI. He began to build their military which produced jobs. His people staged and filmed fake attacks by the Polish people and then showed them in theaters, so the German people would have no problem with Hitler invading Poland. The people looked the other way as he took control, and by the time anyone became alarmed at what was going on in their country, he had control of enough people, so he could use fear to control and manipulate the public. Neville Chamberlain, the Prime Minister of The United Kingdom, was even manipulated by Hitler. After returning from a meeting with Hitler in Germany, Chamberlain stated, "I have returned from Germany with peace for our time." Within a year both France and the UK would be at war with Germany. Hitler needed an enemy, however, to get the German people on his side emotionally as he prepared for war in his attempt to make Germany the Third Reich, which basically means the third great empire after the Roman Empire and the Ottoman Empire. Therefore, he made the Jewish people the enemy. He blamed the loss of the war and the bleak financial condition in their country, on the Jewish people. Many of the Jewish people were financially better off than most Germans, so it was easy for Hitler to make them the face of the enemy. It's called class warfare. Blame the rich. Blame someone, and the people who are not doing well will follow the manipulator anywhere. People in America don't like to think, as intelligent citizens, that they could be manipulated or influenced unwillingly. They will tell you they are independent thinkers. They are educated. And this is America, not Nazi Germany, or the USSR, or Cuba, right? "How lucky for those in power that people don't think." Adolf Hitler

A lot like what happened in Germany, Mao Zedong came along at a time in China when the country was in terrible shape. He and the communist party convinced the Chinese people that their enemy was capitalists, foreigners, and the old Chinese Nationalist Government, again class warfare. China's infrastructure and the economy was in turmoil. He gained the support of the peasants who were struggling under Japanese rule and civil war. Mao also used fear to control and manipulate. He killed over a million landlords who resisted communist rule and consequently met little resistance after that. His policies are believed to have caused a famine that resulted in the deaths of 20 million people, but by then Mao controlled their lives in every way. When things aren't going right in people's lives, they are easily convinced to try something new.

But that can't happen here

"When the people fear the government there is tyranny. When the government fears the people there is liberty." Thomas Jefferson

Once again, this is America. Are Americans really like puppets with someone pulling their strings? Could fear and manipulation cause the people of the country that has been the leader of the free world to lose their faith and love for their country? Could fear and manipulation cause America to have so much turmoil that the public might be open to something different?

Thomas Jefferson said, "If all the American people know all the facts they will never make a mistake." However, do the people know all the facts, is the question.

Josef Goebbels, Adolf Hitler's chief propaganda officer, stated, "If you tell a lie big enough and keep repeating it, people will eventually come to believe it." He went on to say, "The truth is the greatest enemy of the state."

George Orwell, novelist, political writer and journalist, also said, "The people will believe what the media tells them they believe." Most people aren't so concerned about the truth as they are about someone reinforcing what they believe to be the truth.

Sometimes a lie is told so convincingly that even the people telling it begin to believe it. What is a lie? One definition says, an un-truthful statement intended to deceive. Throughout this book, evidence will show how Americans have been manipulated and deceived therefore for a long time by these lies.

Specifically, who is doing this manipulating? And why? What is the big concern about this manipulation? As Hillary Clinton remarked recently when asked about the death of an American Ambassador and three other Americans, "At this point, what difference does it make?"

Liberty and freedom to live someone's life any way they want to, for the most part, has been the keystone of American success. Capitalism gave the people who came to this country the freedom to reach the heights of their ambition if they were willing to educate themselves, work long hours, and take some chances. Basically, freedom to make their own choices about most of their life, to say and do as they please as long as it didn't harm others. One of the biggest choices was the ability for a common person to own private property. For once, these people could work for themselves instead of some tyrant. These manipulators are attempting to take these freedoms and liberties away. In the book, The Protestants by Alec Ryrie, the author explains that Protestants founded this country, and Protestants by nature were people who wanted to be left alone. An idea of limited government was set up to "leave people alone."

America was different in that way. In countries with despotic or socialist governments, sometimes their citizens were told where they could live and what occupation the motherland needed at the time. In some countries, if someone was born into a class, that is where they would spend the rest of their life. If they stood up and voiced their dissent about that despotic government, there is a good chance they probably would wind up in prison or worse. America was the land of freedom and individual choices. America was founded by people trying to escape countries that took away freedom from individuals.

To control skillfully is one of the definitions found for manipulation. So again, who is doing this manipulating and why? In Thomas Sowell's book, Intellectuals and Society, he explained that only a narrow group of "elites" or "experts" are considered intellectuals and consequently qualified for the masses to follow or be governed by. Some might say that the media has become a pseudo-intellectual, to be blindly followed by the masses, rather like a "Judas" goat. For those of you that are younger or not familiar with that term, slaughterhouses, which is another name for a meat processing plant, use goats to lead sheep into the area where they will be killed, thus the term, Judas Goat. Are most Americans being lead like sheep? Lieutenant Colonel David Grossman wrote in his book, On Combat, that people are either wolves, sheep, or sheepdogs. Wolves are predators. They are aggressive and many times violent. They kill sheep or wildlife or whatever for food, but sometimes they kill just for fun. Sheep stand around in bunches and hope for the best. They hope that the wolves will eat their neighbor instead of them. The sheepdogs have some of the same aggressive and sometimes violent nature as the wolves, but they have been taught, indoctrinated, and manipulated to know their job is to protect the sheep from the wolves. Sheep ranchers many times own one or several dogs called Great Pyrenees. This dog, in this case, is not a pet. He is raised with the sheep and fed with the sheep, and the sheep are his family. In many areas where sheep are raised, coyotes or wolves are a problem because they know sheep are an easy meal because they won't fight back. However, a 180 pound Great Pyrenees can change their mind quickly. When you look in the mirror, do you see a wolf a sheep or a sheepdog? Most people are sheep. They follow the herd wherever it goes without question. The sheepdogs are looked down on. That is until the wolves show up. Then they are asking the sheepdogs to protect them.

America has always been referred to as the land of the free. The founders and framers came here from other countries where they didn't have all these freedoms and choices. They wanted to build a system that would ensure those freedoms and choices for the people and they were determined to build a system of government that would have certain guardrails and parameters where no individual or group could take away these freedoms. Several of the founders fought against ratifying the Constitution because it didn't give enough power to the states or the people. Hence, they wrote the Bill of Rights. The Bill of Rights clearly outlines these freedoms. These were freedoms that citizens of other countries merely dreamed about. They were referred to as God-given rights.

1. Freedom of speech, press, religion and petition: Congress shall make no law respecting an establishment of religion, or prohibiting the free exercise thereof, or abridging the freedom of speech, or of the press, or the right of the people peaceably to assemble, and to petition the government for a redress of grievances.
2. Right to keep and bear arms: A well-regulated militia, being necessary to the security of a free state, the right of the people to keep and bear arms, shall not be infringed.

3. Conditions for quarters of soldiers: No soldier shall, in time of peace be quartered in any house, without the consent of the owner, nor in time of war, but in a manner prescribed by law.

4. Rights of search and seizure regulated: The right of the people to be secure in their persons, houses, papers, and effects, against unreasonable searches and seizures, shall not be violated, and no warrants shall issue, but upon probable cause, supported by oath or affirmation, and particularly describing the place to be searched, and the persons or things to be seized.

5. Provisions concerning prosecution: No person shall be held to answer for a capital, or otherwise infamous crime, unless on a presentment or indictment of a grand jury, except in cases arising in the land or naval forces, or in the militia, when in actual service in time of war or public danger; nor shall any person be subject for the same offense to be twice put in jeopardy of life or limb; nor shall be compelled in any criminal case to be a witness against himself, nor be deprived of life, liberty, or property, without due process of law; nor shall private property be taken for public use without just compensation.

6. Right to a speedy trial: In all criminal prosecutions, the accused shall enjoy the right to a speedy and public trial. By an impartial jury of the State and district wherein the crime shall have been committed, which district shall have been previously ascertained by law, and to be informed of the nature and cause of the accusation; to be confronted with the witness against him; to have compulsory process for obtaining witnesses in his favor, and to have the assistance of counsel for his defense.

7. Right to a trial by jury: In suits of common law, where the value in controversy shall exceed twenty dollars, the right of trial by jury shall be preserved, and no fact tried by a jury shall be

otherwise reexamined in any court of the United States, than according to the rules of the common law.

8. Excessive bail, cruel punishment: Excessive bail shall not be required, nor excessive fines imposed, nor cruel and unusual punishment inflicted.

9. Rules of construction of the Constitution: The enumeration in the Constitution, of certain rights, shall not be construed to deny or disparage others retained by the people.

10. Rights of the States under the Constitution: The powers not delegated to the United States by the Constitution, nor prohibited by it to the States, are reserved to the States respectively, or to the people.

The United States Constitution is an amazing document that has helped shape this country, and consequently, has had a tremendous indirect influence on the rest of the world. Thomas Jefferson called the U.S. Constitution, "unquestionably the wisest constitution ever yet presented to men." The U.S. Constitution is the oldest written national constitution in the world. George Washington said "The Constitution is a guide that I will never abandon." The founders were amazing men who put together a document that would protect the people, even from their own government. It was intended to give all the power to the people at the local or state level.

In the "Age of Enlightenment" several European philosophers, Locke, Montesquieu, Voltaire, and Rousseau began to write about and advocate for a different type of government. Historically, countries had been ruled by despotic governments i.e. kings, queens, princes, sultans, dictators, etc. These European philosopher's ideas greatly influenced our founding fathers in designing our Constitution and our system of government. A government where the people are in charge. A government that has checks and balances in place so no one or no part of the government could become too powerful. The framers took all these ideas and worked and fought and argued and finally came up with a document that addressed the wants but also the concerns of men who had experienced the problems with governments or leaders who held all the power instead of the people.

In other words, once again, the purpose of the U.S. Constitution was to limit the power of the Federal Government, not the American people. This had never been done before. English author, Paul Johnson, wrote, "A country specifically created by and for ordinary men and women." The Federalist Papers make this quite clear.

In 1787, the founders saw a need for an executive branch that would have tremendous power, but they also made it clear the president would never be as powerful as the Constitution. The president's job was to be in charge of the army and to uphold the Constitution and nothing more. This would be the first country to set up this type of government. It has been referred to as the American experiment. That idea of limited government is now rapidly deteriorating. The Federal Government is now involved with everything. A recent survey showed that 77% of Americans believe that the Federal Government is controlling the people instead of the people controlling the government. Patrick Henry once wrote, "The Constitution is not a document for the government to restrain the people. It is an instrument for the people to restrain the government." The Constitution is very clear what the Federal Government has the authority to do. The Federal Government was only formed because the 13 states felt like they needed protection from other countries and therefore would need an army. There was never any intention for the Federal Government to be involved in every aspect of the people's lives.

Edmund Burke, an author and one-time member of the English Parliament in the 1700s, stated, "In this character of Americans, a love of freedom is the predominating feature which marks and distinguishes the whole... this fierce spirit of liberty is stronger in the English colonies (America), probably than in any other people of the earth."

Some of the state mottos show the fierce spirit that built this great country and reflects how early Americans felt about liberty.

Alabama: "We dare defend our rights."

Arkansas: "The people rule."

Iowa: "Our liberties we prize and our rights we will maintain."

Massachusetts: "By the sword we seek peace, but peace only under liberty."

New Hampshire: "Live free or die."

Pennsylvania: "Virtue, liberty, and independence."

South Dakota: "Under God, the people rule."

Where have these strong feelings gone? Burke talked about a fierce spirit. Where has this fierce spirit gone? Are these mottos taught in the schools of these states anymore? Complacency, unfortunately, has replaced the fire that once was.

It is all about "liberty." The people who built this country said they were willing to risk all for liberty. Liberty to live the way they wanted. Liberty to believe and worship the way they wanted. Liberty to work as hard as they wanted in order to own their own property. Liberty to live wherever they wanted, even if it meant risking their life to live in wilderness areas. And with this liberty they understood that this much freedom and liberty meant they had to be willing to take other risks, such as the risks to feed themselves, the risks to protect themselves, and the risk to achieve and many times fail. Americans take risks every day. Over 500,000 people jump out of airplanes each year. Over 3 million people are certified to scuba dive. On average ten people per day die in non-boating related (swimming pools) drownings. For a fee, anyone with a driver's license can go to a race track and drive a retired NASCAR 160 mph. Americans have always liked taking risks, but now the elites are telling them that they know better. Liberty is slipping away from Americans today. No one took this liberty away from them, however. They willingly gave up their liberty because the manipulators convinced them that they would be better off. They only wanted just a little bit of their liberty, just enough to keep them safer they said. Karl Marx once said, "Remove one freedom per generation, and soon you will have no freedom, and no one would have noticed." The elites basically said the masses are not capable of taking care of themselves or making decisions for themselves and because of their great intelligence and abilities that they should make the decisions for the masses and a little at a time, the masses said ok. Federal and state governments are telling the people what they can eat and drink. They tell people that they can't ride a motorcycle without a helmet. See, if someone chooses to ride a motorcycle, they are choosing to take some risks in their life, to begin with, and that risk does not cause others harm and therefore is their business! Why is this important? Because it allows someone else to control their lives. There are risks that are also hazardous to others and therefore may need to be regulated.

 People are required by law to wear a seat belt when they are driving their car. The mayor of New York City passed a law forbidding 32 oz. soft drinks. The government has told parents now that they will decide how to raise their children and how to keep their children safe based on their standards, and if these parents don't abide by those standards they will have their children taken away by the state. They are telling the masses how they are to educate their children based on their standards, and after all, being safer is a good idea, right? Who is "they" by the way? Everyone wants their kids to be safer, right? The Federal Government is now regulating what children should eat at school. Vegetables are better than pizza or hamburgers, aren't they? That is just common sense that parents should agree to, right? The problem with children gaining too much weight is not because they are eating grilled cheese or corny dogs at school, its because they are watching television eight hours a day or playing video games, or on Facebook all day instead of riding bikes, playing tag, playing hide and go seek, finding some old boards and building a fort, and climbing trees. This phenomenon of obese children was not as prevalent in earlier generations that ate fried chicken, mashed potatoes and gravy, and bacon and eggs, because their mother wouldn't allow them to even be in the house unless it was raining. Children of those earlier generations helped mow the grass and pull weeds. They didn't have cell phones at six years old, so if they wanted to talk to their friend down the street, they had to walk down there or ride their bike. So why aren't the kids outside? Because of the power of television, parents are paranoid that there are pedophiles waiting on every street corner, hoping those parents will let their children come outside. There have always been predators who wanted to do bad things to children. However, news about these predators wasn't broadcast on every channel 24 hours a day. Fear is a powerful tool in the manipulation process.

Seat belts may not have been the first time the state and Federal Governmen forced people to be safe whether they wanted to or not, but it serves the purpose to make this point. Another way of describing how these elites control people is a term called paternalism. One definition of paternalism states that it is a behavior by a person, organization, or state, which limits some person or group's liberty or autonomy for that person or groups own good. Paternalism or elitist behavior is all about a feeling of superiority. A simple example of paternalism is the regulation in each state that people must wear seat belts. The state, being the parent, telling drivers they must keep themselves safe. If someone rides a bicycle, in many states, they are required to wear a helmet even though the rider has chosen that risk voluntarily. In other words, does going without a seatbelt, or a bicycle helmet, harm others? Is it safer to drive with a seatbelt? Yes, but who decided it was okay for the state or society to act like a parent? The people give up some of their individual liberty every time they tell the government, state, federal or local that its ok for them to control public behavior because it's good for them. Hitler stated, "The best way to take control over a people and control them utterly is to take a little of their freedom at a time, to erode rights by a thousand tiny and imperceptible reductions. In this way, the people will not see those rights and freedoms being removed until past the point at which these changes cannot be reversed." It's like the old story about how do you cook a frog? You increase the temperature ever so slightly, and the frog will swim around not noticing until the water is boiling, and then it's too late to escape. Life is a risk, and with freedom there is a risk. Certainly, buckling that seat belt would be safer in most cases than choosing not to wear it, but that is not the government's business. That should be left to the individual if they choose to take that risk. Shall the government force everyone to wear helmets and flack vests while they are driving? Let's force the automakers to only build cars out of rubber. Closing swimming pools would save lives. Banning motorcycles would save lives. People are killed every year because of snow skiing, rock climbing, scuba diving, boating, flying, skydiving, riding bicycles, and sometimes just walking across the street. Smoking takes millions of lives, and there are a lot of people who would like to ban cigarettes. Although most Americans find smoking offensive, it is not the government's business if someone chooses to take that risk. Adverse reactions to prescription medications kill millions. Shall we ban prescription meds? So why do the politicians only choose certain risks to try and control? They choose the ones they can get away with. They choose the ones that they get lobbied or paid to choose. Remember, turn up the temperature a little at a time, and soon you have complete control.

When the people tell any government entity that they are not capable of taking care of themselves, they become children to a tyrannical form of government that the founders fled their home countries to avoid. "We are fast approaching the stage of the ultimate inversion: the stage where the government is free to do anything it pleases, while the citizens may act only by permission." Ayn Rand

Montesquieu wrote about the need for separation of powers and consequently, the need for three different branches, Executive, Legislative and Judicial. He strongly believed that each of these branches should hold the other branches in check. In, Democracy in America, he wrote, "If the legislative power is united with the executive power in the hands of one person, or of any one body of officials, there can be no liberty, nor can there be any liberty if the power to judge is not separated from the legislative and executive powers." The U.S. Constitution gave authority to the three branches of our government to govern, support, and manage, but not to control society. The framers of the Constitution were very concerned about any one branch of the government becoming too strong or having too much authority. Therefore, the judicial and legislative branches were given very specific tools as countermeasures to a possible overbearing executive branch and vice versa. Today the executive and legislative branches of the government plant people into the judicial branch as well as the now fourth branch, the regulatory branch, to control and manipulate the processes and the daily lives of Americans in many ways. Regulatory branches of government such as the Environmental Protection Agency, The Department of Homeland Security, and the Consumer Protection Bureau, just to name a few, are completely out of control. Since 9/11, terrorism and national security have become a top priority in America. However, the governments answer to every issue of "more is better" is evident when you look at the ludicrous additions of personnel and buildings that have been added to supposedly keep the public safe. An investigation by the Washington Post showed that there have been 1,271 government organizations and 1,931 private companies added since 9/11 to work on programs related to counterterrorism. The Department of Homeland Security now has a workforce of 230,000. And there are now 854,000 government employees with "Top Secret Clearance." Major General John M Custer, the Director of Intelligence at The U.S. Central Command commented about part of this behemoth at The National Counter Terrorism Center, when he stated in an interview, "After 4 ½ years this organization has never produced one shred of information that helped me prosecute three wars."

 The Environmental Protection Agency is currently asking to increase their budget, so they can increase their personnel from approximately 18,000 to 230,000 people. Have another issue, just create another agency. According to The Daily Caller, the U.S. Government does not know how many agencies and programs it is asking taxpayers to fund.

 The legislative branch, on both sides, plays a game that resembles a scripted professional wrestling match. It's like they have a meeting over coffee, and one side tells the other side, "Okay, you propose this idea, and I will act indignant and pound my fist and go on television and tell the public I won't stand for this, and then later we will compromise." As mentioned previously, in the first 100 years of this country, most people elected to Congress or the Presidency were business owners. They served a few years, and then went back to their farm or business. Rather than serve a term or two, today our congresspeople focus on what will get them re-elected each term, hopefully forever, instead of focusing on what is good for our country. In fact, some people who are wanting to get elected will sometimes change parties if they feel like they will have an easier road that way. They can't rock the boat. They can't truly speak their mind because being too judgmental or too hard-lined on an idea might cost them some votes in the next election. The few politicians who do stand up and speak their mind are labeled extremists. In the past few years, politicians and those that promote certain politicians, have learned to use the concept of politically correct, to manipulate. Standing up and speaking your mind, telling people that you think an issue is wrong, might offend someone, so the rule of the day is to just keep your mouth shut. Or when asked a question, a politician will completely change the subject or just talk about their cause. In the past, there was a term called the silent minority. Today, because of politically correct its changed to the silent majority. A few people who are referred to as squeaky wheels, and their trial lawyers, are making most of the decisions in this country, even though the majority of Americans may disagree with those decisions. Find an issue that 3% of Americans believe in, and then find the right trial lawyer, have the mainstream media do some emotional stories about it, and all of a sudden the other 97% are having to abide by new rules, and they are told by the media that most Americans believe in these new rules. Absurdity has become the new normal.

The Korean symbol called a Ying Yang refers to balance. For a long time having a two-party system in America seemed to keep things balanced. Republicans kept Democrats from going too far one way, and Democrats kept Republicans from going too far the other way. That's not the case any longer. Democrats don't give an inch because they know most of the Republicans are more worried about the next news story and the next election and therefore won't stand up and fight. The silent majority also tends to just go along with whatever is happening. They may not be happy with some of the changes in our country that go against what they believe, but if they have a job, get to take a vacation each year, were able to buy a big screen TV, and a new car, they don't get all worked up. Just turn off the television if its bad news. Recently a presidential candidate lied about having to duck and run because of gunfire when she landed in Bosnia. This was later found to be a lie. When reporters asked some young people, who said they would vote for this candidate, what they thought about her lying, they responded, "all politicians lie." Sports teams are caught cheating. Yet the fans still fill the stadiums and arenas. Hollywood celebrities or music artists are convicted of beating up their wife or girlfriend, but their admiring fans still show up for their concerts and still watch their movies. The younger generation is being taught that right and wrong don't matter. All that matters is what you can get away with.

Professional politicians, with the help of different areas of the media, have manipulated the feelings and therefore the thinking of the American public for a very long time and by stirring people's emotions, consequently, they didn't get a lot of flak when they went around some of the restrictions put on them by the Constitution. Amy Goodman, a broadcast journalist stated, "Journalism is the only profession explicitly protected by the U.S. Constitution because journalists are supposed to be the check and balance on government. We're supposed to be holding those in power accountable, asking the critical questions. We're not supposed to be their megaphones. That's what the corporate media have become." There are three main network television stations in America, and they truly have become the megaphones for the Democratic Party.

One definition of the word manipulated is to influence others for personal gain. Personal gain can come in many forms. In most cases, the personal gain that results, is control and power. But it can also be extreme wealth. Recently, the head of General Electric was appointed by President Obama to be his Chairman of the Outside Panel of Economic Advisors, whatever that means. Is it a coincidence that NBC, which is owned by General Electric, was so supportive of this President? Sometimes this manipulation by these politicians was for personal gain, but many times it was for personal differences in the philosophies or ideologies that Margaret Thatcher talked about. Politicians usually get involved in politics because of an ideology or a particular issue that they are passionate about. However, after some time has passed they learn how to use these ideologies as a tool to persuade and manipulate their following.

Although the list can go on and on to show all the ways that Americans have been manipulated, the focus of this book will be to address some of the main areas that are affecting the country today.

 The first topic is how the office of the presidency has become far too powerful. The U.S. Constitution is by far, the best document and therefore best system of government on our planet. Whenever one man, as in the president, has so much power, inevitably egos become a driving force in their decisions, and currently our Constitution does not have enough roadblocks to keep these power-grabs from happening. If people went by the "letter of the law" so to speak, our Constitution would keep any one branch of the government from becoming too powerful. The recent administration has shown however, that there are ways around things if no one objects. Throughout American history, many presidents have made decisions that affected the American way of life and in many cases cost lives to leave their legacy. After all, if you're the president, do you want to be listed in the history books as the president who did nothing? This power becomes a narcotic for some. Imagine being referred to as the most powerful man in the world. Wouldn't you want to exercise some of that power? Think about the kind of person who wants to be the President of the United States. Someone who thinks they are smarter and more capable than the other 300 million people in America. That's an ego. Through someone's experience, if they show that they have some experience that would be beneficial in this office, then that experience should help them earn their way into the presidency. This hasn't been the case in the past couple of decades. The presidency has become a popularity contest. And the party that promotes the winner then puts this person on a pedestal as an all-seeing, all-knowing, and all-powerful individual that "runs" the country. The framers of the Constitution were very worried about this happening. They insisted that the Constitution should hold all the power, not any one man. Frank Herbert Jr, the author of the science fiction stories, Dune, once stated, "All governments suffer from a recurring problem. Power attracts pathological personalities. It is not that power corrupts but that it is magnetic to the corruptible."

Looking at other countries, many wonder how their governments could become so corrupt. It's because of power, control, and sometimes money. Money is a good thing. Capitalism is a good thing, but money derived by giving favors to cronies is one of the main causes of a corrupt government. This is happening in both parties, by the way. Large corporations sometimes support certain politicians because those same politicians will give them exemptions from onerous regulations or help with tax issues. A construction company that wants to build a dam will contribute millions to a campaign of someone they know will use their influence, once elected, to get appropriations for that dam in the proper area.

At this point some other words related to manipulated may cross your mind, such as indoctrinated, coerced, fooled, misled, or a rather slang term used a lot during the cold war years, brain-washed.

All you need are some soundbites to stir people up. Just say things like "a war on women," or "finally equal pay," or "black lives matter," or just words like "racism," "bigoted," "white privilege," or "military style assault weapons." Words like these naturally stir up emotions and make people bristle.

Manipulation is easy when all one hears is one side of the story. Pravda, a Russian newspaper, made sure Russians only heard one side of the story for decades to control their people's thoughts and opinions. Because they were spoon fed certain stories, Russians believed that capitalism was evil, and that Americans wanted to bomb Russia, and therefore Russia had to be prepared to fire back. The manipulators here however, are much more subtle. The media has tremendous influence over the public's perception and therefore actions. Hollywood celebrities side with liberals about gun control, yet they make millions making movies that are filled with gun violence. They side with liberals about the war on women, yet again they make millions on movies with explicit sex scenes and nude women which sell tickets. Social media has now become very influential all over the world. Young people especially, who are looking for something to believe in, something to be passionate about, or some way they can help to change the world, are sometimes caught up in movements and protests, and because of their youthful passion, they become involved with matters without knowing the facts. Someone sends out a "tweet" that hey we're all going downtown to protest...whatever. The internet has so much information, but too many times people don't bother finding out what is true and what is false, what is fact, what is just someone's opinion and what is just gossip. There's a saying, "The truth will set you free." Hearing the truth sometimes will make you mad. First, you'll be mad because you won't believe the truth, then later, you'll be mad because of how you were lied to and how you were manipulated.

 Most parents remember the frustration of how often their children asked, why, why, why. Children don't just take things for granted. In a recent Google commercial, it was noted that an average child asks 144 questions per day. Children question everything. Somewhere along the way, however, adults quit asking why? Instead, most people listen to so-called authorities, experts, political leaders, and all the various forms of media, and just assume what they are saying must be true and correct. If this information is written in a book, newspaper, magazine, or reported by a news anchor on a major TV network, then the masses tend to take it as gospel. Especially, if they feel like life is not going the way they want, they tend to look for something that will make things better. They look for someone to follow. They look for information that fits their agenda or plight. November 18th, 1978, Jim Jones, a self-proclaimed messiah who preached equality and socialism, instructed his followers to give cyanide-laced punch to their children and then themselves. Over 900 people, including 276 children, died that day because one man knew how to manipulate their thinking and consequently their actions. In Oregon, the Bhagwan Rajneesh persuaded followers to sell everything they owned and give him all the proceeds and join a commune, which thousands did. The Bagwhan, however, didn't follow his teachings. When he was deported from the U.S., he owned 75 Rolls Royces. History is filled with unusually very charismatic individuals who were masters at manipulating their followers.

Drones

Thomas Sowell explained in his book, Intellectuals and Society, that only a narrow group of experts are considered intellectuals and consequently qualified for the masses to follow or be governed by. Mark Levin also talked about these elite individuals in his book, Liberty and Tyranny, and that these elites really believe they are superior and that they should be making decisions for the masses. America's framers came from countries where despotic leaders such as kings, queens, dictators, sultans, and caesars told their subjects what rights, if any, that they were allowed. America was to be a different country. Different from any country there had ever been. A country where the people decided their future, not a king or some other monarch. In America, the people were to be in charge of the politicians instead of the other way around.

Celebrities of all kinds, actors, comedians, or sports figures, with the aid of electronic media, also have an enormous amount of influence, especially on our young people, sometimes because they are held up as experts, and sometimes just because they are well-liked, handsome, cute, or talented. Why do you see celebrities in commercials? Do you really think Drew Barrymore shops at Wal-Mart? One quick anecdote, When my mother was in her mid-80s, she remarked to me that she didn't like Republicans because they wanted to take away her Social

Security. I asked her where she got that information, and she replied: "Katie, on TV, said so." Hollywood has learned to use people's emotions to affect their thinking and consequently their actions. In the past two years alone, there have been three movies about how people were discriminated against in the past. Most Americans would like to forget about race, but Hollywood won't let them. Want Americans to worry about global warming? Just make several "end of the world" movies and within a short period, electric car sales go up. Movies about the mistreatment of the American Indian, the mistreatment of horses, and mis treatment by police, pull at everyone's heartstrings and make them angry. Recent television commercials portrayed a Republican congressman look-a-like, pushing an older lady in a wheelchair, over a cliff. Therefore, Republicans must be bad people. They want to push granny over the cliff. Oh, that makes me mad. I can't believe Republicans are so heartless. They don't care about old people. George H. W. Bush pledged to not raise taxes. The predominant Democrat congress persuaded him because of the debit, he must agree to raise taxes. So in an attempt to work with them, he agreed. Then when he ran for re-election, the Democrats repeatedly showed commercials of President Bush saying, "Read my lips no new taxes." He raised taxes because of the pressure from the democratic congress and then the Democrats used it against him. Voters got mad at him, and therefore, with the help of a Ross Perot bid for the presidency, Bill Clinton defeated George H. W. Bush. Make people mad, and they will vote. More on that later.

If it's on television or in writing it must be true

The same television network that persuaded my mother that Republicans were against old people, recently helped stir up an incident by selectively editing a 911 call, so it appeared that what happened in an incident in Florida with a young black man named Trayvon Martin, was racially motivated. Within days the Black Panthers, Jesse Jackson, Al Sharpton, and half of Hollywood were demanding justice. Protests and marches took place in many cities which inflamed the situation. The network admitted that one of their employees had edited the 911 tape, but the flames of racism had already been ignited. President Obama even made comments concerning the case. When the facts came out about this case and the Department of Justice ruled that race was not the issue the same television station never mentioned that. This station had spent days trying to convict a man of racism related murder yet when the truth was revealed they barely mentioned their "mistake." The president never acknowledged that maybe he overreacted. The comedian who put out the address on Twitter, of the man accused who was found innocent, never apologized. After a young armed Black man was shot by a black police officer in Milwaukee, the young man's sister called for violence against white people even though her brother who was armed, was shot by a black police officer. She called for the violence to be taken to the suburbs. CNN, however, edited the story to look like the woman had called for peace instead of violence.

Recently, the Blaze reported that Representative Corrine Brown a Democrat from the Fifth District of Florida, who after professing in an interview to "care about all the children" who fall victim to murder, could not remember the name of a little girl from her district who was murdered and then dumped in a Georgia landfill. She couldn't remember Somer Thompson's name, but she had no problem recalling what she thought she knew about the Trayvon Martin issue. There are thousands of minority shootings and stabbings in this country every year, but because of an edited tape, the Trayvon Martin issue became one of the most publicized stories of the year. Two years later, politicians and the media are still insinuating that this was a racially motivated killing. In another case in Ferguson Missouri, a young black man named Michael Brown was shot and killed by a white police officer. A friend of the young man who was killed claimed that his friend was on his knees with his hands in the air asking the policeman to not shoot, and that the policeman basically executed him. Ten witnesses of which seven were black, said this never happened. They stated that the young man fought with the policeman over his gun, and then later charged the policeman and was shot as he charged. The forensic evidence supported this testimony. Even though all evidence showed that the hands-up scenario never happened, activists like Al Sharpton, along with politicians and celebrities still promote this story and protestors years later are still walking the streets holding their hands in the air shouting "hands up don't shoot". A protest in New York City included a large crowd shouting, "What do we want, dead cops? When do we want it? Now.

The President sent the Department of Justice to investigate the Michael Brown incident. The president and the Attorney General held press conferences to talk about how racism, has to be addressed. Even after the Department of Justice said there was no evidence to support the hands-up story, President Obama and his Attorney General still did not back off. Protests and riots happened in each of these incidents because politicians and the media reported things that weren't true. In both cases, a young man was killed which was a tragedy, but eyewitnesses in both cases disputed the racial claims as the reason for the young men being killed. In 2014 Colleen Hufford was sitting at her desk in a business in Oklahoma City when a young man who had converted to Islam walked in and attacked her while he yelled "Allah Akbar". He cut her head off with a knife, and then attacked another woman and was trying to sever her head before he was shot by the owner of the business. This story was talked about for a few days by the media, but was soon forgotten. Ask most Americans who Trayvon Martin or Michael Brown were and most will be able to tell you. Ask Americans who Colleen Hufford was, and ten out of ten will not be able to answer. The media keeps the stories in your head that they want you to focus on.

 It's easy to manipulate someone's thinking, just leave part of a story off or if a manipulator wants to use statistics he or she just finds the statistics that fit their story.

Years ago, liberal politicians said something must be done to do something about the discrimination in the mortgage and banking industry because blacks were turned down for a loan twice as often as whites. That was a true statement but is only part of the story. The rest of the story, however, was that whites were turned down twice as often as Asians and that black-owned banks turned down blacks twice as often as whites, but those facts were omitted. Manipulators are cunning and know how to use the part of the story and maybe the facts and figures that fit their agenda.

When does a theory become a fact? Charles Darwin's theory of evolution has been taught more as fact instead of theory for decades. Evolution theory states that humans evolved from apes. Some scientists are now questioning that theory. After all, there is no evidence of a missing link and no evidence that any creatures have continued to evolve. Yet this theory is taught in our public schools as fact. Since 1960 we were taught that our solar system contained nine planets, and students would certainly have to be able to name them to pass a science test. Now scientists have decided that Pluto is not a planet. For decades, margarine was sold to the public that it was much healthier than butter but now there are studies that show that it may not be as healthy as once thought. Aspartame is an FDA approved sweetener used to replace sugar in soft drinks and various other products because sugar is bad. Flies will avoid it, yet the government says its ok for American's to consume. And just recently there have been studies that say cholesterol may not have anything to do with heart disease anyway. Could the big push to use margarine instead of butter have anything to do with how much money was contributed to the American Medical Society by the vegetable oil industry? Manipulating people is so easy. Beef is bad for you, eggs are bad for you, coffee and alcohol are bad for you until another study is done showing just the opposite. Stay out of the sun. No wait, you need some sun. How many times today is there a commercial on television advertising a great new prescription medicine that treats a particular medical problem, only to see attorneys a few years later advertising about lawsuits concerning the same medicines?

John Lennox stated, "Nonsense is nonsense, even when it is spoken by famous scientists." Global warming became a religion, so to speak a few years ago, thanks to Al Gore and a whole list of celebrities and politicians. This is a theory that claims that the earth is warming and that the reason for this increase in temperatures is humans producing too much CO2. The theory is that cars and industry are the two main culprits, but humans using too much electricity are also bad people. Al Gore credits his science professor, Roger Revelle, as the one who taught him that global warming was caused by human beings. Later when Revelle changed some of his thinking about global warming, Gore commented that Revelle was senile. The icebergs are melting, and therefore Polar bears are having to swim great distances to find something to eat and also to find some ice to get on. The truth is, Polar bears can swim 50 miles, and there are more Polar bears alive today than there has been in 50 years. Recently, when the U.S. experienced some of the coldest winters on record and it was also noted that the Antarctica was actually getting thicker instead of thinner, the name for this man-made catastrophe was changed to "climate change." Global warming no longer fits the story. There are thousands of scientistswho believe this theory and thousand who do not. Dudley J. Hughes, a retired geologist and author, of Geologic Reinterpretation of the Earth's Atmospheric History, wrote in an article in Environment and Climate news in 2007, that CO2 makes up less than 1% of the Earth's atmosphere and has no negative effect on the Earth's environment. In the early 70s, there were a group of scientists who proposed a global cooling theory and warned of the next ice age on the way. Newsweek magazine had an article titled "The Cooling World" but then in 2008, Newsweek magazine published an article titled "Global warming is a cause of the year's extreme weather." And just recently, The Washington Post reported that we may be entering into a mini ice age. So why is global warming so important to the democratic agenda? Over the years the Democratic Party has leaned more and more towards a socialist platform where people are more and more dependent on the government. Driving small economical cars, or not driving at all, and living in urban areas and relying on mass transportation will reduce the carbon footprint according to the climate change believers. However, these ideas would tend to put people into the same box, much more than they are today. Socialism proposes that the masses should be equal. People who drive big SUVs and live in large houses in the suburbs make poor socialists.

What is a theory? One definition says, "a proposed explanation whose status is still conjectural and subject to experimentation, in contrast to well established propositions that are regarded as reporting matters of fact." What is conjectural? One definition says, "of the nature of or involving conjecture, problematic, speculative." What is problematic? One definition says, "The nature of a problem, doubtful, uncertain, questionable." In other words, a theory is someone's opinion. It's not called a law or a fact, it's a theory. However, this theory is treated as fact, not theory. Could this be for someone's personal gain? Hollywood movies that promote this theory receive grants. The green industry is a multi-billion-dollar industry and the facts and why politicians need this deception will be discussed a little later. The advocates of these theories don't think about and in reality, don't care about the consequences of their actions because their belief that their cause is just. If thousands of Americans lose their job because of these unproven theories, oh well.

 Theories, beliefs, paradigms, all shape people's thinking and consequently their actions. Between TV, radio, social media, and the internet, the public is bombarded with information that attempts to move them to action.

When one reads or hear this information, how are they to know what is fact and what is someone's opinion or theory?

 Instead of following along with the "herd" we the people should go back to asking why. Why are certain laws passed? Why do politicians side with one point or message and then change and advocate for an opposite point? President Obama once said, "I don't believe in gay marriage. You shouldn't mess around with the constitution. Just because two people that care for each other want to get married." Later when he changed his position, he said he had evolved. It's about control. Who is trying to gain all this control and why?

"Government even in its best state is but a necessary evil. In its worst state, an intolerable one." Thomas Paine

Remember the Maine

This is an example from over a century ago of how the media was able to influence the actions of Americans. In 1895, Cuban rebels were fighting against Spain for their independence. Cuban dissidents were put in concentration camps, and hundreds of thousands died. Many Americans, politicians, and media, were sympathetic to their cause. After all, America was a relatively new independent nation, shouldn't the people in Cuba have the same opportunity?

During this time, two newspaper magnates, Joseph Pulitzer and William Randolph Hearst were feverishly competing for dominance of the newspaper world. Whoever could come up with the biggest stories sold the most newspapers. Sometimes it didn't matter if the stories were true, as long as people believed they were true. A term referred to as "yellow journalism" was coined to point to some of these stories that were sometimes exaggerated, embellished, or sensationalized and sometimes completely fabricated. One such story had a great impact on America going to war with Spain in 1898. Hearst even sent Frederick Remington to Cuba to paint images of what he saw. By 1898, American and Spanish relations were at an all-time low. Hearst somehow found a letter that had been written by the

Spanish minister to the United States, criticizing President McKinley. He published the letter on February 9, 1898. A patriotic America was infuriated by this insult.

The USS Battleship Maine sailed into Havana harbor on a friendly and protective mission. They were there to protect Americans in case the Cuban conflict became violent. On the evening of February 15th, 1898, shortly after 9:00 pm, a mysterious explosion occurred on board the USS Maine, which was anchored in the harbor. The explosion resulted in the Maine sinking rapidly, and 266 American sailors lost their lives. A brief inquiry by the Navy concluded that the explosion must have been caused by a mine placed beneath the ship. However, there was some belief that the explosion was due to an accident. The media was quick to blame the explosion on some type of torpedo or mine. Hearst's and Pulitzer's papers did their best to inflame the situation, insinuating that it must have been sabotage and therefore it must be the Spanish. In Hearst's New York Journal on February 17th, 1898, an editorial stated, "The removal of the Maine meant a tremendous reduction in the odds against her in the event of the conflict that all Spanish Havana desired. The chances against such a removal by accident were millions to one, and yet the removal occurred. In such, polite expressions of regret count for nothing. The investigation must clearly disclose Spain's innocence, or her guilt will be assumed." The editorial went on to say, "Whether a Spanish torpedo sank the Maine or not, peace must be restored in Cuba at once. We cannot have peace without fighting for it, let us fight and have it over with."

The American public, already upset by the stories of inhumane treatment of Cuban prisoners by the Spanish, were quickly enraged about a possible attack on one of America's ships. There was no proof that Spain had sabotaged the Maine, but with the help of some persuasive newspapers Americans had already made up their minds. President William McKinley, reacting to the public fervor, went to Congress on April 11th and asked for permission to intervene in the conflict and subsequently ordered a naval Blockade of the Havana harbor. The next day Spain declared war on the United States, and on April 24th the U.S. followed with their own declaration of war. Spain wasn't prepared for a war with the U.S. The Spanish-American war only lasted six months with America achieving victory and helping Cuba gain their independence and also liberating Guam, Puerto Rico. and the Philippines in the process.

 President McKinley had recently appointed Teddy Roosevelt as the Assistant Secretary of the Navy. Although he had been ordered to only blockade the Philippines, convinced that war was inevitable, Roosevelt ordered Commodore George Dewey to intercept the Spanish fleet in Manila Bay. The anchored Spanish fleet was destroyed. Roosevelt once said, "I should welcome almost any war, for I think this country needs one." He felt like war was purifying and helped young men show their mettle. This was the opportunity Teddy Roosevelt was looking for. The war propelled him into the public spotlight and on to becoming our 26th president. Teddy Roosevelt is remembered as leading a charge of soldiers referred to as the "Rough Riders" up San Juan Hill. The headline, "Remember the Maine" was printed in papers across America and reportedly also became a battle cry amongst those soldiers.

The newspaper stories of the Maine's sinking that helped take us to war were, completely false. It was discovered after an investigation in 1976 by Admiral Hyman Rickover that the explosion on board the Maine was the result of an accident caused by internal combustion of coal in the boiler room which was adjacent to the ammunition room on the ship. Rather poor planning of a ship's construction, don't you think? The main's demise was self-inflicted according to Admiral Rickover. Did anyone bother to do a thorough investigation before printing the sabotage story? With the media, typically whoever breaks the story wins, so to speak.

Why? Could it be that two newspaper magnates held beliefs that Cuba should be free, so let's do something to help this cause? No one can say what was in the head of these two men, but the stories they printed, as well as other newspapers and magazines, did have a great impact on the feelings and consequently the actions of the American people and leaders. Was this just one mistake or could this have happened again? This has happened throughout America's history and happens on a regular basis today.

Who are "They"?

"There are three kinds of men. The one who learns by reading. The few who learn by observation. The rest of them have to pee on the electric fence for themselves." Will Rogers

Then there are those who take whatever they hear on TV or read in the newspaper as truth, without questioning it. Every day people hear something like, "they say," "studies show," or "an informed source reports." They say margarine is better for you. They say that Polar Bears are disappearing. They say that Americans are the unhealthiest people on earth. So, who are "they?" For many Americans, their only source of information is the three major television networks, ABC, NBC, and CBS. Other sources that are taken at their word are, The New York Times, CNN, Fox News, The Huffington Post and for Latinos, Univision. Whether they listen to the morning or evening news or one of the late morning news programs, the news they hear is the news that these TV stations want them to hear. And it really isn't the "news" anymore. It is entertainment and ratings. And persuasion is what it is all about. The people on these news shows are commentators giving their opinion, not journalists reporting news. In the past, these media sources supported the liberal politicians, but now they are leading the liberal politicians.

When someone defends themselves with a firearm, it is never reported on the "news." Very seldom are there any positive stories reported on the news programs.

People are so easily influenced by the media and politicians or hear-say. "They say" gets repeated over and over. They say that Republicans are supported by Wall Street and the large corporations. However, Hillary Clinton, a recent Democrat presidential candidate received $675,000 for giving three speeches to "Wall Street." They say that strong hurricanes are caused by global warming, yet the worst hurricane in history was more than 100 years ago. They say everyone should have a swine flu shot. Yet the effects of swine flu are less than regular flu. They say that the oceans are rising, yet Al Gore bought an ocean view property in 2010. They say you should drink milk. They say you shouldn't drink milk. They say that cell phones will give you cancer.

Most people's favorite sitcoms, dramas, or sports programs are on the main network channels so even if someone has some conservative beliefs they can be heavily influenced by constant liberal-leaning stories or opinions thrown at them sometimes through seemingly harmless commercials or characters in their favorite show.

The interviewers on these news programs are also masters of knowing what questions to ask to get their guest talking about subjects in the way the interviewer directs. If at some point the guest tries to take charge of the conversation, the interviewer will quickly interrupt or change the subject. The recent Presidential debates are a good example of this. Liberal-leaning cable stations are another source of one-sided information intended to persuade people to think a certain way, such as

MSNBC. Some would say that Fox News would also fall into this category on the conservative side. However, Fox seems to be turning more liberal also. National Public Radio, which is subsidized by tax money, approximately $90 million per year, criticizes conservative ideas or conservative people even though they should be impartial. Internet search engines like Google and AOL show liberal-leaning headlines and stories when someone turns on their computer. Young people who spend much of their day on the internet are heavily influenced by what they see and hear on the internet and social media. Talk radio has become a huge phenomenon in America mostly dominated by conservatives. However, six different conservative talk shows give six different opinions about the current news or issues. The liberal station hosts tend to be on the same side of the issues with each other almost every time. Their message is clear, Republicans are bad people. Republicans are bigots. Republicans want dirty air. Republicans are just for the rich people and corporations. Many others get their information from headlines on the front of a magazine at the grocery store checkout counter. The National Enquirer boasts a circulation of over 2.7 million. These tabloid papers tend to focus on sensational crimes or stories that involve sex or celebrity gossip. During a presidential election, however, gossip stories involving sex and possible cult involvement were headline news on the front cover of several tabloids. And unfortunately, with many people, all they have to do is read a headline or see an incriminating photo to believe the gossip. After all, they couldn't print it if it weren't true, right?

Why do the main television stations and most of the newspapers in this country tend to lean toward liberal thinking? They are all owned by liberals.

Americans react to stories they hear on television or read on social media and the internet whether they know the stories are true or not.

A lie doesn't become truth, wrong doesn't become right, and evil doesn't become good just because it's accepted by a majority.

Every President needs a war

If you want to be remembered in the history books, you need to fight a war or two, right?

Like Teddy Roosevelt, Lyndon Baines Johnson, better known as LBJ, knew that. He wanted to be remembered for lots of things. He did not want to be remembered for being the President that lost Vietnam. He stated, "If we quit Vietnam tomorrow we'll be fighting in Hawaii, and next week we'll be fighting in San Francisco." President Johnson's major impact on America will be discussed again later.

President Dwight Eisenhower was concerned about the communist influence in Southeast Asia and consequently in 1955 sent 16 military advisers into South Vietnam to aid the South Vietnamese Army with tactics. He was convinced that if Vietnan fell under communist rule that one by one all of the countries in Southeast Asia, and even the Philippines, would probably fall also. Eventually, he would have 700 advisers in Vietnam. President John Kennedy followed this plan but increased the number of advisers and special forces to 16,000. After a tense time in October when the Russians attempted to move missiles into Cuba, JFK was very concerned about the communists. However he had mixed feelings about U.S. involvement in Vietnam because he felt the South Vietnamese leadership was incompetent, and he had even considered withdrawing all of the advisers. LBJ however, like Eisenhower, thought it was up to America to curb the flow of communism. And then after a horrible day in November 1963 on the streets of Dallas when President Kennedy was assassinated, Lyndon Baines Johnson became the President and inherited the Vietnam situation. LBJ would have more influence on the future of America than probably any President since Abraham Lincoln. He was a powerful and cunning politician. He knew how the system worked better than anyone. He wanted the communists to go away. In early 1964, Johnson started "Rolling Thunder," an extensive bombing campaign. In March of 1964, Robert McNamara, Johnson's Secretary of Defense, reported poor results so far in Vietnam. Prior to the 1964 election, LBJ told the American public that he would not send American troops thousands of miles overseas to do what the South Vietnamese should be doing. His ideas about that soon changed. Johnson wanted to escalate our involvement, but he knew he would need congressional and public approval. His opportunity came on August 2, 1964, when the USS Maddox opened fire on three North Vietnamese patrol boats when they came too close. The Maddox and supporting U.S. aircraft caused heavy damage to the opposing patrol boats. The North Vietnamese patrol boats responded and fired torpedoes at the Maddox but missed their target. Then, on the night of August 4, 1964, Captain Herrick of the USS Maddox reported another attack. Later that day LBJ went on national television and reported that the North Vietnamese had attacked two of our ships on the open seas and he also told America of his intention to retaliate. On August 7th, Congress passed the Gulf of Tonkin resolution authorizing LBJ to take all necessary measures to repel any armed attack against the forces of the United States and to prevent further aggression. Several of the major news magazines all ran articles describing the attacks. President Johnson ordered retaliatory air strikes against North Vietnam, and by July of 1965, he would send 44 combat troop battalions there. Eventually, 550,000 Americans would be sent to Vietnam and 58,000 would die and thousands would become severely disabled as a result. The war in Vietnam would be called a conflict or a police action instead of a war. Why? Could it be that a certain political party didn't want to be known as the party that took America to war, but instead simply was standing up for the defenseless South Vietnamese? And since it wasn't officially a war, our military wasn't allowed to win it. Air Force pilots reported being given orders to drop their bombs in the open ocean rather than on enemy targets. Political correctness raised its ugly head and would become a precursor to most political decisions as well as part of American daily lives ever since.

In an NSA report released in 2005, according to CIA Director John Mc Cone when asked did he think the North Vietnamese attacked our ships because they wanted a war, McCone responded, "No, the North Vietnamese are reacting defensively to our attacks on their offshore islands...The attack is a signal to us that the North Vietnamese have the will and determination to continue the war." The attack on August 2nd did occur. LBJ conceded in a private conversation with McNamara that the attack was provoked by a classified attack on the North Vietnamese, called "Operation Plan 34B." Regarding the second attack, in a recorded conversation, LBJ remarked to his Secretary of Defense Robert McNamara, that he doubted that the attack on August 4th ever happened. He remarked, "Hell, those damn stupid sailors were just shooting at flying fish." Regarding this second phantom attack, Historian Robert J. Hanyok studied the records of this incident and reported that the attack on August 4th did not happen, but Johnson and

Mcnamara used the claim to support retaliatory air strikes and to buttress the administrations request for a Congressional resolution that would give the White House freedom of action in Vietnam. Over the next few years, LBJ would refer back to the Gulf of Tonkin incident and almost unanimous vote in order to get support for increased action and increased budget requirements.

Why did this President use this bogus intel of a phantom attack? So that he would have a reason to take America to war? LBJ was a powerful leader and ruled the Senate with an iron fist, and when he became the President of the United States of America, which has been referred to many times as the most powerful man in the world, could it be that he wanted to show his power? He commented three weeks after the Kennedy assassination that he couldn't lose in Vietnam. Later as the war became very unpopular at home, he remarked to Senator Eugene McCarthy in February of 1966, "I know we oughtn't to be there, but I can't get out." He went on to say, "I just can't be the architect of surrender." This was one of the first times that television had a major impact on American ideas about war. Suddenly stories about Vietnam along with sometimes graphic photos showed the reality of war. Thousands of people, especially young people, began to voice their dissent about the war. Protests became news also, which fueled more dissent. The war became very unpopular with more and more Americans as the number of deaths accumulated, especially when returning soldiers and Marines told stories about how they weren't allowed to win. Some of the liberal media began to run stories about atrocities by the American military that mostly came from hearsay. Several celebrities used their celebrity to try and influence the public and in many cases, were condemning

America and siding with the North Vietnamese. All wars tend to lose their luster as time wears on, and Vietnam was no exception. So, as the war became more and more unpopular, the more momentum the enemy gained. President Johnson decided not to run for re-election in 1968, therefore leaving the problem to Richard Nixon. He also left an enormous amount of debt to Nixon which most believe is the reason Nixon had to take America off the Gold Standard, to keep the foreign debtors from taking all the gold that America owned. After the war was over, some North Vietnam military leaders commented that they knew they couldn't defeat the American military, but they figured out that they just had to hold on and the American media would win the war for them.

LBJ was known to have extremely liberal, bordering on socialist, ideas. So why would he be so concerned about communism in Southeast Asia? Or was he more concerned about the USSR or China becoming the dominant superpower? Or was it the narcotic of power mentioned earlier? Just 90 miles away from the U.S., Castro had turned Cuba into a Communist tyranny along with help from the USSR. Why wasn't LBJ concerned about that communist influence?

If LBJ was so anti-communist, why did he present the Medal of Freedom to Edmund Wilson in 1963? Edmund Wilson was an author who voted communist or socialist in every election. Phyllis Schlafly wrote in her book, "A Choice Not An Echo," that LBJ also gave an award that included $50,000 to J. Robert Oppenheimer. Oppenheimer was known to be contributing substantial sums to the communist party. Why did LBJ arrange to sell millions of bushels of wheat to the Russians at a bargain price? Why did LBJ either ignore or support communism all around him but felt that he needed to send thousands of American young men to Vietnam to fight and die to stop the communist take over there?

This war took 58,000 young American lives who were just doing what their country asked them to do. Hundreds of thousands more became disabled in many ways, and America became more divided than at any time since the civil war. Why?

The buck stops here

A Scottish historian, Sir Alex Fraser Tyler, wrote in 1801, "A democracy cannot exist as a permanent form of government. It can exist only until voters discover that they can vote themselves largesses from the public treasury. From that time on, the majority always votes for the candidate promising the most benefits from the public treasury..."

"The buck stops here" was a famous quote of President Harry Truman. It was supposed to refer to the idea that responsibility always would ultimately find its way to the President. However, this saying could probably be attached to numerous presidents, but in a different context. It could also be said that the buck stops here saying, has to do with ever increasing revenue. And it's always under the guise that it is going to help America. President Woodrow Wilson believed strongly that the government was the answer to all problems and therefore to fix all the problems in America, the government needed lots of bucks. In 1913, the 12th amendment was passed allowing the Federal Government to impose an income tax. Americans were told that this would simply be a tax on the wealthy, the Rockefellers and such. And in fact, it was, at first. The top tax rate was 6% and was only imposed on people who earned over $250,000 per year. In 1913 there were few of those, so why would the masses object? Why should an average American worry about a tax on the wealthy? Today approximately 50% of Americans now pay a substantial portion of their earnings into the government coffers to do with as the government wants. The top tax rate has been as high as 94% during World War II and 70% during the Carter administration and is now at 39%. At the time this book was written, the Federal Government has now built up over $22 trillion dollars in debt, so it's a given believed by most, that taxes will rise in the near future. That is not the whole story, however. There is another 7.8 trillion dollars in liabilities that are not accounted for that are for federal employee benefits, another 23.8 trillion dollars in additional obligations for Social Security, and another 27.3 trillion dollars in additional Medicare obligations. These funds are in addition to the revenues generated by payroll taxes. This results in a massive shortfall. Numbers from justfacts.com show that this shortfall means that every person living in America owes $224,110 to the federal debt. Some economists say that this is not a major concern because we have had this level of debt to GDP before such as during WWII and we came out of it just fine. Before the Obama administration, the federal debt had never exceeded more than 70% of the Gross Domestic Product. By the end of his term it exceeded 102% of the GDP. The biggest concern by all Americans is about this debt is that 47% of it is owned by other countries and specifically China, which owns 26% of our debt. What would happen if America can't pay the debt to China? The vast majority of Americans believe the level of debt is a major problem. Yet the out of control government keeps increasing their spending as if the issue would just magically fix itself someday.

FDR is known by many to be the president that cared about the common man. During his administration, the idea of the Federal Government taking care of the public really took off. He instituted Social Security, which is now being referred to as Federal Benefit Payments as if the government actually produced this money. Social Security was an insurance program that was put in to place to help people with their retirement. Or was it? Social Security was signed in to law in 1935 by FDR and started in 1937. The qualifying age to receive Social Security benefits at that time was 65. The average life expectancy in 1937 was somewhere between 58 and 63. How many people did they really think would receive benefits? The few people that received a benefit from Social Security at that time usually only collected it for about two years. In the 40s for every 40 people that were paying into Social Security, there was only one person receiving benefits. FDR promised that the Social Security program would always be voluntary, which everyone knows it no longer is. He also promised that the participants would never pay more than 1% of the first $1,400. Now all employees pay including Medicare and Medicaid, 7.65% of everything they make up to $118,000 and employers match that. The money contributed would be deductible from one's federal income tax and not only is it not deductible any longer, we are now taxed on up to 85% of the benefit. The money was always supposed to be put into a special trust fund and not used for anything else that the government wanted to use it for, but LBJ changed that and put it into the general fund. Who made all these changes? The Democratic Party took away the tax deduction. The Democratic Party moved the money from the trust fund to the general fund, and in addition, the Democratic Party ultimately under Bill Clinton made the benefits taxable. However, the spin heard on the mainstream media, is that the Republicans want to take Social Security away and throw granny off the cliff. So, who was this influx of revenue helping? Social Security was a huge cash cow for the government to use if they needed it. Now for every person that's receiving benefits, there are only two people paying into the fund. The average male currently has a life expectancy of 83 and the average woman, 85. Over 100,000 centenarian birthday cards are sold each year now. Social security will have to be fixed or the money allocated will run out starting in 2033. The Social Security board of Trustees states that as of 2033, the two so called trust funds will only be able to pay out .75 on the dollar of benefits. Most senior citizens are happy they have a Social Security check, and it has now become an integral part of most people's retirement income. Or are they just conditioned? What if there had never been a Social Security system? As stated earlier, out of each paycheck each person pays 7.65% into the Social Security and Medicare system. The current median household income in the U.S. is approximately $49,000. Median means that half of the households make less than that and half of the households make more than that. This is typically a more accurate picture than average income. People like Warren Buffet, Bill Gates, and Alice Walton, tend to skew the numbers if you use averages. Currently, the Social Security percentage is 6.20%. Just to keep things simple, if you take that $49,000 median income times 6.20%, and lets say this person or couple works for 45 years then that equals $ 136,710. Would this person be better off had they kept that money and made maybe 3%-5% on their money over those 45 years? Galveston County in Texas opted out of the social security system many years ago and chose instead to build their own system. The Galveston County employees proportionately receive higher benefits than other Americans. The country of Chile built a similar system to Social Security but they allowed the money to be invested privately and proportionately their system outperforms the U.S. system also. The possibility of this happening in America is slim and has caused many heated discussions in Washington, as well as the kitchen table.

First, it was Welfare, and Medicaid. Now there is also food stamps, Wik, housing aid, subsidized health care, free cell phones, and so on, and so on. Recently another presidential candidate was campaigning on the idea of free healthcare and free education. Nothing is free! Someone has to pay for these things. Free stuff is not a new idea. LBJ's ideas of giving out lots of freebies was called the Great Society. Was LBJ's great society a way to help people or control people? Alexis de Tocqueville wrote, "The American Republic will endure until the day the Congress discovers that it can bribe the public with the public's money." Colonel Allen West remarked, "When more Americans prefer freebies to freedom, these great United States will become a fertile ground for tyranny." That's never been more evident than today. Illegal immigration has become one of the top issues in the country. Milton Friedman said you can't have open borders if you have welfare. Welfare attracts people from the rest of the world that many times are not interested in coming here to work or to build a business, they are simply coming here to let someone take care of them. The Syrian so-called refugees are signing up for federal assistance as soon as they arrive. The cost of this assistance is over $67,000 per year per person. Before the U.S. borders became so porous the majority of immigrants came here because of job opportunities, not welfare. Why is there money to pay for these refugees but not cost of living increases for Social Security?

From about 1896 until 1964, the Democratic Party claimed to be the working man's party. However, it was the white protestant working man's party. That all changed starting in 1964. The democratic machine which had been anti- black, anti- latino, anti-anything basically but white protestant, figured out how they could control the minorities and consequently control their vote. Give them a monthly check, and you'll control their vote no matter what color their skin is. But the Democrats were specifically targeting the black community and now also the Latino community with this so-called help. And that manipulation is working well because today blacks vote over 90% for Democrats and Latinos over 60% Democrat.

 LBJ's welfare programs were sold as programs to help the poor, especially these minority segments of our population. Have they helped? Have they improved life in America for minorities? There are more people in the minority communities in poverty today than before these programs were implemented. This was an orchestrated movement that was started by Richard Cloward and Frances Fox Pivens. The Cloward –Piven plan intended to overload the welfare system to the point where it would collapse, and therefore the government would provide a guaranteed income payment for all. Thomas Sowell stated, "No society ever thrived because it had a large and growing class of parasites living off those who produce."

Thomas Jefferson remarked about the same issue, "The democracy will cease to exist when you take away from those who are willing to work and give to those who would not." The progressive politicians want especially minority neighborhoods dependent upon the government and once they are dependent it is very difficult to change that behavior.

Why are there minority neighborhoods at all at this point? Did someone want to keep Blacks or Latinos from mingling or living next door to white Americans? Could welfare help keep those neighborhoods segregated? Did LBJ feel superior to the less fortunate and feel the need to take care of people that he felt were not able to improve their own situation by themselves, or did he see this as a way to control a segment of the population and therefore control their vote? His history shows the latter. Before LBJ's Great Society, most Black families had a father and a mother in the home that were usually married, they went to church, and for the most part, were employed. In fact, before welfare, Black families were more likely to have both a father and a mother in the home than Whites. Before welfare, many Blacks started their own businesses. In 1964, Black babies born out of wedlock averaged 16%. Forty-seven years later, our poverty rate has not improved. Now 72% of Black babies are born out of wedlock. Latino out of wedlock births are over 60%. In comparison, White out of wedlock births are at approximately 29%. The current welfare system promotes illegitimacy. In an article in National Review on 8-21-2013, Michael Tanner reported a single woman receiving $15,000 in welfare per year would also receive about $5,200 per year in food stamps, but if she marries a man who receives about the same annual income, her food stamps would go to zero. Another example, a single mom receiving about $20,000 per year who marries a man making about the same amount would typically lose about $12,000 per year in benefits. Welfare was supposed to be a temporary hand-up to help people in poverty, however, there are little incentives for someone to get off welfare. Michael Tanner went on to report that in Hawaii a person would have to earn in excess of $60,590 per year to be better off than welfare. On the site, Discover the networks.org,

Heritage Foundation scholar Michael Franc noted in 2012, "welfare recipients who enter the workforce or receive pay raises, lose a dollar or more of benefits for each additional dollar they earn." From the same article, in testimony on Capitol Hill, Rep. Geoff Davis, R-Kentucky, concurred that "although federal welfare programs are designed to alleviate poverty while promoting work, collectively they have an unintended side effect of discouraging harder work and higher earnings." Rep. Gwen Moore D-Wisconsin, a former welfare recipient, acknowledged in her oral testimony, "I once had a job and begged my supervisor not to give me a .50 per hour raise lest I lose my Title 20 daycare." So how does that affect the Black family? Welfare has replaced the economic need for a second parent in the home. Fathers play a key role in the development of morality and work ethic with young men. Robert Rector reported on 11-17-2014, in an article titled, "How welfare undermines marriage and what to do about it." He showed that without a father in the home young people were twice as likely to be arrested for juvenile crime, and they were twice as likely to have emotional and behavior problems. They were twice as likely to be suspended or expelled from school, and they were about one third more likely to drop out of high school before completion. So where do these young men get the positive influence of working hard and taking care of their family? It was also noted that the poverty rate for America for single-parent homes is approximately 35.6%, but the rate for married couples is only 6.4%.

Prior to welfare, Black men did not make up the majority of our prison population. Today, although Blacks are approximately 13% of the population, the proportion of Black men incarcerated in our jails and prisons is approximately six times as high as Whites, and Latinos are three times as high as Whites. Prior to LBJ's welfare system, the proportions of incarcerated men and women closely followed the overall population proportions. Previous CBO Director, June O'Neill showed in a report that increasing the time that a child spends on welfare may decrease their IQ by 20%. Her report showed that welfare doubles the probability that a woman will have a child out of wedlock and doubles the probability that a boy of any color will become a threat to society, or wind up in jail. The FBI reports that the ratio of assaults of Black on White or White on Black is 50-1 Black on White, and the ratio of murders is 14-1 Black on White. Overall, Blacks are 7 times more likely to commit murder than Whites. Latinos are 6 times more likely to murder than Whites. Blacks are 15 times more likely to be gang members than Whites and Latinos are 16 times more likely to become gang members than Whites. The highest crime/ murder rates in America are all in the urban areas of Chicago, New Orleans, Washington DC, Baltimore, Atlanta, and Los Angeles, coincidentally each of these cities have been run by Democrats for decades. These terrible murder and crime rates are not the fault of White people, or the Black society either. They are the fault of Democrats and policies kept in place to keep minorities segregated and dependent. Blacks have been voting in Democrat leaders for 60 plus years and their situation has not improved. A study by Mary Corcoran and Roger Gordon at the University of Michigan showed that receipt of welfare income has a negative effect on the long-term employment and earning capacity of young boys. And when young boys can't find a job they will find something else to do.

In a 1996 report by Patrick F. Fagan and Robert Rector, they stated that marriage is economically irrational in the welfare society.

Is there still some racism in America. Yes there is. There will always be some Whites that don't like Blacks, Blacks that don't like Whites, Mexicans that don't like Blacks, Cubans that don't like Puerto Ricans, or whatever. However, some of this racism is disguised, and some can be blamed on welfare. The welfare society has been devastating to young Black men, the main people it was supposedly intended to help. The murder rate in America of Black men killing other Black men is horrific. Estimates show that over 300,000 Black men have been killed by other Black men over the last 35 years. The unemployment rate for young Black men is over 40% in most areas of the country. The mainstream media never cover these issues because it doesn't fit their story. The mainstream media want Americans to continue to believe that White people are inherently prejudiced and somewhat bigoted, (unless they are Democrats). Blacks killing other Blacks isn't a major story, and therefore it is ignored by the media and the Democrats. In 1960, prior to welfare these problems were nowhere near as bad as they are today. Today if a young Black youth spends much time reading and trying to improve themselves, they are told they are acting White. Where does that come from? If a Black becomes a conservative politician or spokesman, they are called Uncle Tom, or they have abandoned their people. Where does that come from? An ESPN reporter stated that an NFL quarterback wasn't Black enough because he was married to a White woman and he was a conservative. Just understand where this at least partially comes from, the people who make their living by keeping racism alive. As mentioned before, Blacks are 13% of the American population, but 39.8 % of welfare recipients are Black. This is not an attack on Blacks or Latinos. It is actually the opposite. This is an attempt to open some eyes of people in the minority communities to realize who is manipulating you for their benefit. See, most Black people are good people. Most White people are good people. Most Latinos are good people, and by the way, most cops are good people. There is a current movement called Black Lives Matter which is a group that supposedly was started to protest police shootings of Black Americans. The leftist politicians and the mainstream media have thrown their support behind this group. Apparently Black lives only matter to the leftist politicians and liberal media when it fits their agenda, however. When a nine-year-old Black girl is shot and killed while she is doing her homework, in a drive-by shooting in a minority neighborhood, it is hardly mentioned on the three main network television stations or gets limited exposure in any of the liberal newspapers. In Chicago, Tyshawn Lee, 9 years old, was lured into an alley and executed because his father was in an opposing gang. Where was Al Sharpton then? Why wasn't Jesse Jackson calling for protests and investigations? Why didn't President Obama make a big deal out of this tragedy? Why didn't Eric Holder call for a federal investigation? Why didn't some celebrity tweet the address of the gang out? When a Black man executes a young White reporter and her young cameraman because of race, again its hardly mentioned or the story reported by the media has to do with gun violence rather than race. When a Black man walked up behind a young White girl on Sunset Strip in Hollywood and shot her in the back of the head for no apparent reason, the mainstream television stations didn't give this story two minutes. Omar Thornton. Does that name ring a bell? Probably not. His story got limited exposure for a few days.

August 3rd, 2010, Omar killed 8 White people where he had worked. He called 911 and explained it was a racist place, and he wished he had got more. Why wasn't this a big story? When a partly White man kills a 19-year-old Black man, the mainstream network television stations repeatedly showed pictures of the young man when he was 12 years old. When this incident happened, this young man was 6'3 and 190 pounds but the mainstream television stations continually showed pictures of him as a young boy and people got upset. That's manipulation. When a White police officer shoots and kills a Black man, the mainstream television stations and liberal newspapers have stories for weeks and sometimes months. And when these television stations talk about these events with a liberal slant that vilifies the shooter, most of the time before all the evidence comes in, then emotions take over and facts don't seem to matter anymore. The facts are that cops are six times more likely to be killed by a Black man than Black men are to be killed by cops. Many are not willing to hear the truth because the truth damages their cause. Earlier we showed the statistics of Black on White crime, yet if you listen to the people that have an incentive to keep the racial fires going, you would think there is a mass of murders by Whites and White police officers on the Blacks in America. Are there some bad cops? Sometimes there are, and when they go bad, they need to go to jail just like any other criminal. There are over 800,000 police officers in this country and the great majority of these people put their life on the line every day and do their job properly. The people in this country would all be in trouble without them.

This concocted emotion about race is destroying the progress that was experienced in America the last fifty years, and it's dangerous. This hate rhetoric has recently resulted in the ambush and murder of eight police officers. These officers who were doing their job, as a matter of fact, five that were working a Black Lives Matter protest at the time, were assassinated because someone bought into the lie that cops are killing young Black men left and right because they are Black. Recently a Black Muslim leader asked for 10,000 Black men to stand up. He stated that if the Federal Government won't stop their problems, then they would have to stop it themselves, they would have to kill the people who were the problem. The same leader called White people devils. These people are pouring gasoline on a racial fire and re-opening old wounds that were on the way to becoming a smaller and smaller issue in America.

Human beings have historically done very ugly things to each other. The Germans were responsible for the deaths of six million people, mostly Jews, in World War II. Should the Jews hold that against all the German people today? Dr. Ben Carson stated in a recent presidential debate that Americans are not enemies of each other. The enemies are the people trying to keep us divided. Some of the ways they keep us divided are very subtle. Promoting television shows or entire television stations that are all Black, or constantly announcing that this man or this woman is the first African American to do this or that or having organizations that supposedly advocate for Blacks or Latinos, keeps us divided. Herman Cain was a Republican candidate for President in 2012. He said, "Don't call me an African American. I'm not from Africa. My father or mother nor my grandparents were from Africa. I'm not a Black American. I'm just an American."

This attitude hurts their cause. Should a White person refer to themself as an English, Irish, Scottish American, or a White

American, or just Heinz 57? Like Herman Cain said, they should just be an American.

The current welfare system in America is in great part responsible for young minority children dropping out of school and being on the streets and many times becoming pregnant at 15 which keeps the not enough parenting culture alive in those neighborhoods. How does a 15-year-old or 16-year-old girl raise a child or sometimes two or three children? According to the US Department of Health and Human Services, in 2013 there were 273,105 births by teen mothers between the ages of 15-19. Almost 89% of these births were out of wedlock. One in six of these young mothers had more than one birth before age 20. BlackDoctor.org states that 23% of 14-year-olds have had sex. By race, 17% of teens between age 15-19 have had a child before age 20, 16% for Blacks and 8% for Whites. Children born to teens statistically have more health problems and more education and behavioral problems. Of all unplanned pregnancies of this age group, 60% resulted in a live birth, 30% were aborted, and 15% resulted in a miscarriage, again according to the U.S. Department of Health and Human Services. The truth is that the welfare system especially cripples the minority family and keeps them from being able to excel and achieve and experience opportunity.

Much in the same way this system cripples much of the Native American population. Henry Ford stated, "Any man who thinks he can be happy and prosperous by letting the government take care of him, better take a closer look at the American Indian," Some of the highest murder rates in the United States are on reservations. Alcoholism and diseases like diabetes are destroying Native American families and culture. The White man conquered the American Indians over 100 years ago, much like civilization after civilizations have done for thousands of years all over the world. However, that same White man told those Native Americans, move on to the reservation and we will take care of you. Currently, the Bureau of Indian Affairs has over 9,000 employees who are supposed to take care of the people on the reservations. Yet these people are among the poorest people in America. Reservation land is held in trust by the Federal Government and therefore the people that live there are not allowed to own their home. People living on reservations are among the least educated in America. The high school graduation rate on reservations is just slightly above 50%. The reservations are a lot like the Black and Latino areas of our urban cities. They are all told, stay here Black man, stay here Mexican, stay here Native American, and we will take care of you. This is not an original quote, but there is a group of people in this country that want to keep people on the plantation and the reservation. Why? As long as these segments of the American population are kept in these circumstances, their vote is assured to go to whoever promises them the most freebies.

Just like LBJ's selective anger toward the communists, he apparently looked at civil rights in the same selective ways, i.e. what was politically advantageous for him at the time. The U.S. Senate, which was led by LBJ, fought to stop civil rights laws from being passed in the 50s. Later, when LBJ became President, and his advisers told him he needed to change his position he suddenly became the champion of civil rights acts. This change in attitude was for political purposes not because LBJ suddenly developed a conscience.

By 2011 ,38.9% of Whites are also receiving some form of welfare which will cripple and make dependent most of those families also. A hand up is a good thing, but an orchestrated plan to keep certain segments of our society dependent on government is a terrible injustice.

Former Secretary of State, Condaleeza Rice wrote, "If you are taught bitterness and anger, then you will believe you are a victim. You will feel aggrieved, and the twin brother to aggrievement is entitlement. So now you think you are owed something and you don't have to work for it, and now you're on a really bad road to nowhere because there are people who will play to that sense of victimhood, aggrievement, and entitlement, and you still won't have a job." You need to understand if you are dependent on the government, they want you to stay that way. The Democrats are not trying to help you, they just want your vote. Some Republicans are also not trying to help you, they just want your vote. The media is currently trying to convince the minority communities that Republicans have changed their spots and are now equivalent to the southern Democrats or Klu Klux Klan. There is no evidence to support this but all they have to do apparently is state it on the network news shows, and it becomes fact. The evidence shows the opposite. Look at the voting records, folks. Look at the facts. Look at all of the big cities in the U.S. that are struggling financially and have the highest crime rates that have been run by Democrats for decades.

Food, housing, and medical care costs have risen sharply in the past 15 years, but typical income has lagged far behind. This trend can't keep going like this.

As long as this trend and this system continues on this path, the political party that promotes it will be almost assuredly receive the majority of the votes from this group regardless of their race. President Kennedy once said, "The best form of welfare is a good paying job." Again, who is welfare helping, the low-income people in these neighborhoods or the politician wanting to control their votes?

 In Spanish, the word "Patron" means someone that you work for, but also someone that takes care of you, the master. The Democrats who put these welfare plans together have become the Patron of the minority communities. There needs to be a great awakening in the minority communities to see how they have been duped for years.

Want to talk about racism? Doctor Alveda King, the niece of Martin Luther King Jr, said, the most obvious practitioner of racism in America today is Planned Parenthood. She also stated, "The great irony is that abortion has done what the Klan only dreamed of...roughly ¼ of the Black population is now missing." The left claims that Planned Parenthood helps the minority community. Dr. King claims that in 2008, seven Planned Parenthood offices were contacted and offered donations for aborting Black babies. The caller would say there are way too many Blacks in America. In every case, the Planned Parenthood offices were willing to take the donations. I mentioned that sometimes racism is disguised. Margaret Sanger, the founder of Planned Parenthood, was a believer in Eugenics. Eugenics is the practice or plan that certain segments of the human-race are unfit and should be eliminated. In an article, Sanger wrote, "The Eugenists, for instance, are seeking to assist the human-race toward the elimination of the unfit."

Adolph Hitler was also an advocate of Eugenics. Sanger also remarked, "Eugenics is the most adequate and thorough avenue to the solution of racial political and social problems. Sanger wrote on page 47 of her book, "What Every Girl Should Know," that the "Australian Aborigine, the lowest known species of the human family is just a step above a chimpanzee in brain development with little sexual control." She also remarked, "Through Eugenics we can create a garden of children instead of a disorderly back lot overrun with human weeds." She deemed poor Black babies as "degenerative and defective." She praised Nazi sterilization policies and was a proponent of the Klu Klux Klan and forced sterilization. In 1921 she spoke at a KKK rally and afterward was offered the opportunity to speak at 12 more of their functions.

It wasn't just Blacks that Sanger wanted to control, she believed that anyone such as soldiers, or anyone who was mentally challenged or physically challenged, or poor, needed to be eradicated. In her Birth Control Review publication in 1933, she stated that "Slavs, Latin, and Hebrew immigrants are human weeds…a dead weight of human waste." Is it a coincidence that the first Planned Parenthood clinic was built in Harlem and today 79% of Planned Parenthood clinics are in predominantly Black and Latino neighborhoods. As mentioned before, Blacks are 13% of the U.S. population, however they account for 36% of abortions. On average, there are 850 Black babies aborted every day in the U.S. In 2012, there were more Black babies aborted than born in New York. Oh, but the word baby brings up too many emotions. They are now referred to as fetuses or sometimes tissue, not babies. No one gets upset about aborting a fetus, but killing babies is altogether different. Dr. Ben Carson said, "We've distorted things to the point where people believe that anyone who opposes mothers killing their babies is waging a war on women. How can the public be so foolish to believe such a thing? One must be able to recognize the depravity to which America has sunken as a society when valuing a baby's life is frowned upon." Today the liberal left praises Margaret Sanger for her heroic vision. By the way, Hillary Clinton who was a Democrat candidate for president, said in a speech in Houston Texas that "she admired Margaret Sanger enormously, her courage, her tenacity, her vision." Hillary went on to say, "I am really in awe of her. And there are a lot of lessons we can learn from her life and the cause she launched and fought for and sacrificed so greatly." Feminist organizations have recently proposed putting Margaret Sanger's picture on our ten dollar bill. Sanger had a vision all right. She believed, like Hitler, that there needed to be one master race and even then, the entire human population needed to be reduced by about 80%. In her Birth Control Review publication in April 1932, Sanger stated, "Birth control must lead to a cleaner race." Democratic Supreme Court Justice, Ruth Bader Ginsburg stated, "At the time Roe (Roe v Wade) was decided, there was a concern about population growth and particularly growth in populations that we don't want to have too many of." The message that these people profess that they want to help minorities is a lie. Again, Planned Parenthood and welfare are ways to control minorities, and they are some of the worst cases of manipulation in American history. In 2013, there were 429,000 abortions on Black women. For every three Black babies born, there were two aborted. The progressives have been trying to control the Black population since the Civil War. Abortion is one of their key tools.

"So, who really are the racists?' Derryck Green, a conservative writer, And commentator, asked.

Derryck pointed out that Affirmative Action was implemented under Richard Nixon (Republican) in 1970. Conservatives are accused of being racists because they oppose affirmative action. He went on to say that affirmative action actually hurts many Blacks that had standards lowered for them, so they could attend schools that they are not prepared for and therefore have high drop-out rates. He points out that the same thing would happen to Whites if put in that situation. Affirmative Action is condescending to the Bblack society. It basically is saying that Blacks are not as smart as Whites and therefore need some extra help. One of the problems with Blacks and education is that they are required to attend the schools in their neighborhood which historically have very poor results. Republicans have advocated for school vouchers for some time that would allow these Black students to go to the school of their choice, but Democrats have fought this idea because of the teachers unions.

Another area Derryck talked about is voter ID. Liberals say that requiring voter ID is a way for conservatives to keep Blacks and Latinos from voting. He talks about how condescending that is, again basically saying Blacks are not capable of getting an ID. In Mexic,o every voter is required to have an ID. In India every voter is required to have an ID to vote. In Europe, every voter is required to have an ID.

This is just one more way to try and keep minorities thinking that liberals are their champions.

 There is documented case after case where Democrats aided by the mainstream media have convinced minorities that they are their saviors and supporters, when in reality, they are the ones who have kept minorities from improving their situation. Race is not what segregates America. Culture is what has segregated Americans of different colors, and the dividers want it that way. If they keep minorities poor, then they keep them angry, and as long as they keep them angry, they control their vote.

The ten poorest cities in America are;

1.Detroit, hasn't elected a Republican Mayor since 1961

2.Buffalo, hasn't elected a Republican Mayor since 1954

3.Cincinnati, hasn't elected a Republican Mayor since 1984

4. Cleveland, hasn't elected a Republican Mayor since 1989

5. Miami, has never elected a Republican Mayor

6. St Louis, hasn't elected a Republican Mayor since 1949

7. El Paso, has never elected a Republican Mayor

8. Milwaukee, hasn't elected a Republican Mayor since 1908

9. Philadelphia, hasn't elected a Republican Mayor since 1952

10. Newark, hasn't elected a Republican Mayor since 1907

All these cities have something in common. Every single one of these cities have been run by Democrats for a long time. The poor keep electing Democrats, and they are still poor.

Sometimes this was the result of bad laws, sometimes it was orchestrated. To the people in these minority neighborhoods, you have been duped. You have been lied to and manipulated by people who want to keep you down because they know they will keep your vote that way. We have all been duped, just in different ways. These Democrat leaders, plus the Jesse Jacksons, Al Sharptons, and Louis Farrakhans are Judas goats to the Black society. These people have become wealthy by promoting their hate agenda. Al Sharpton owes $4 million dollars in Federal Income taxes. Ever ask how did he make all that money? "There is a certain class of race-problem solvers who don't want the patient to get well, because as long as the disease holds out, they have not only an easy means of making a living, but also an easy medium through which to make themselves prominent before the public." A quote by Booker T. Washington.

Blacks have been segregated in certain parts of big cities since FDR was president. Why? Black children are segregated to attend the poorest schools in these same neighborhoods. Why?

So again, who really are the racists?

What does this have to do with revenue? Taxes, Taxes, Taxes, and payoffs. The so-called race advocates get huge donations from the largest corporations in the U.S. The race advocates basically extort millions from large corporations who "contribute" to their causes so Al won't be protesting on their front door.

The estimated budget for welfare in 2014 was approximately $654 billion dollars. Taxes are a tool of control. Our taxes help fund Planned Parenthood. Planned Parenthood contributes to the Democratic politicians who continue to promote them. Hillary Clinton currently receives the highest contribution. Approximately $500,000,000 is given to Planned Parenthood each year as a subsidy, therefore our tax dollars help support this slaughter which is disguised as help for minority women to have access to mammograms and annual checkups. Planned Parenthood does not perform mammograms. Fifty-one % of Planned Parenthood's revenue comes from abortions.

Minimum wage is another way of increasing revenue for the government. Although people working for minimum wage usually don't pay income taxes, they do pay Social Security taxes and their employer matches it. So, if the minimum wage increases then revenue increases. And does it really help? When the 17 year-old boy sacking your groceries gets a raise because minimum wage went up, then the baker and the grocery store must increase the cost for a loaf of bread. It's all about revenue and unions. Many unions have a contract clause that requires automatic wage increases for their members anytime there is a raise in minimum wages therefore these unions hire professional protestors to carry signs, etc., in front of McDonalds and Wal Mart. Approximately 2.8% of the working population work for minimum wage. Many of these people are teenagers working their first job. In fact, over 50% are less than 22 years old. A minimum wage job gives young people a start in the business world, so they can learn what it's like to have responsibility. Senator Barack Obama voted against raising the minimum wage, but President Obama was for raising the minimum wage. Today, many low-income workers are immigrants who struggle with the English language, and because our state and local governments have required education to be bilingual, and because companies have learned that marketing in Spanish pays off, these people are held back from finding better paying jobs. However, many of these people came from places where they were making 25 cents per hour, and therefore, if they are getting $8 per hour for flipping burgers they are relatively happy. Raising the minimum wage will help keep workers from trying to improve themselves so they can find a better job. Many of the supervisors and managers at the places that pay minimum wages started out there themselves, but because they didn't want to stay in that situation, they worked hard and therefore were promoted and even in some cases they wound up owning some of the franchises that hired them. Alvaro Urbana went to work sweeping floors at a McDonalds in San Jose, California and worked his way up to the store manager, and in 2009 received the Ray Kroc award for being in the top 1% of McDonald's managers. After spending some time in gangs, Alvaro commented that McDonald's saved his life. Thomas Sowell said the elitists in this country want people to believe they are condemned to stay in their economic or cultural position, but this is America, just ask Alvaro.

January 14, 1987, the New York Times ran an editorial that stated that the right minimum wage was $0.0. They believed there shouldn't be a minimum wage. The editorial remarked that raising the minimum wage would price poor people out of the job market. Now in 2015, the same newspaper is advocating a $15 minimum wage. Los Angeles passed their own minimum wage laws. For 2016, the minimum wage in Los Angeles went to $10 per hour, and it is proposed to go to $15 per hour by 2020. WalMart has decided to close their store in downtown Los Angeles. How many people will get put out of a job because of minimum wage increases?

There has always been a success formula in America; get a high school diploma at least, don't go to jail, get married, don't have kids until you are married, and work hard. Welfare in most cases works against that formula. Do some people need help? Absolutely, but it has been proven over and over that the private sector, and local and state governments does a better job supplying that help than the Federal Government does. The current welfare system and ideas about bilingual education and minimum wage, tend to remove the incentives to better oneself.

This is not a Black, White, or Brown issue. Whether you are Black, Latino, or whatever, do you really want to be segregated from the rest of society because of the color of your skin? Do you really want someone to take care of you like you're not capable of taking care of yourself? Do you really want someone saying you are not smart enough or capable of succeeding because of the color of your skin? The Judas goats want you to stay right where you are. A quick anecdote. In an earlier career, a young Black man who was an employee of a company that I was the manager for, had to take some time off because he was shot while sitting on his front porch. When he returned to work, he explained to me that he heard gunshots in his neighborhood almost every night. It doesn't have to be that way. In America, you can get out of whatever situation you are in, but you first must recognize your situation. Thomas Sowell who was mentioned earlier, dropped out of high school and was a self-proclaimed Marxist. After a few years of hunger, he decided to change his situation. He began to read and learn and not just accept what he was being told. Thomas went on to become a college professor, one of the most recognized economic experts in the country, and a best-selling author. Dr. Ben Carson recognized his situation and realized if he didn't change his situation, he would probably die young. He also began to read and learn. Dr. Carson became the top neurosurgeon in the world and recently was a candidate for president. I was privileged to meet a young woman who lost 72 members of her family in the genocide in Ruanda in 1993. She didn't like her situation, so she changed it. She recognized that Ruanda needed a good body shop, so she read and learned and started a body shop and now employees 23 people.

The buck stops here should mean personal responsibility, but that attitude is quickly changing.

The buck stops in Washington. Is that what Truman really meant?

What is the Fed? The Federal Reserve is a partially privately owned central banking system that was set up in 1913 by some of the richest families in the world including the Rockefellers. The supposed purpose of the Fed is to manipulate the different parts of the United States banking system and consequently our economy. This is done by setting long and short-term interest rates and printing currency, supposedly for the purpose of combatting inflation and providing stability to our financial systems. This is referred to as Monetary Policy. The main tool of Monetary Policy is Open Market Operations. Through this tool, the Fed will print money and usually buy Treasury Bills or bonds. By pumping more currency into the banking system, it artificially inflates our stock market, which is happening currently. The Fed prints currency and then charges the U.S. interest for that currency. Each and every time one of the congressmen or senators proposes a bill to Audit the Fed, it is either voted down or usually never comes up for a vote. The Fed families now own significant portions of ABC, NBC, and CBS and therefore control what might be said about this issue. This also answers the question of why the main network stations support liberals. America has no idea about this manipulation, and when a well-meaning congressman tries to expose it, millions are spent to defeat that congressmen in their next election.

The Fed is keeping interest rates down supposedly to help our economy grow. However, look at what is one of the biggest expenses of our government. The interest paid on our debt in 2017 was approximately $191 billion dollars. The Fed keeps interest rates low, or that number would increase substantially.

This manipulation by the Fed is supposed to help. But look at what happened when President Herbert Hoover used this to tighten the money supply in the Great Depression. Herbert Hoover ran as a Republican and became the 31st President. However, he agreed with the progressive ideas of Teddy Roosevelt's Bull Moose/ Progressive party. Between the panic and resulting massive sell off in October of 1929 of an over-inflated stock market, many consumers lost their life savings. Banks went under because they had backed margin accounts that couldn't pay off. President Hoover decided to restrict the money flow and keep prices high, so corporations would be able to continue to manufacture. However, if consumers can't afford what is being manufactured then they quit buying, and inventories pile up. Then to make things worse, President Hoover and Congress passed the Smoot-Hawley Act which greatly increased tariffs on imports. His thinking was that imports needed to be reduced so there would be more American jobs. The Europeans resented this and therefore implemented their own tariffs, and foreign trade came to a stop. Congress raised the highest rate of personal income tax from 25% to 63% and raised the corporate tax by 15%. The result of these decisions caused unemployment to rise to 24.9%. During this same time frame, a drought in the Mississippi Valley, and what was reported as poor farming practices, caused the Dust Bowl era which put numerous farmers out of business, and in many cases off their land. Not only were millions of Americans out of work, millions were homeless.

President Franklin D. Roosevelt continued most of President Hoover's policies but named these policies, The New Deal. He stated that there was no need to re-invent the wheel that Hoover had already paved the way. The New Deal was supposed to help America out of the depression. But the truth is that until World War II, there was no significant improvement in unemployment or our overall economy. Being at war required new manufacturing which produced jobs, and the war also opened foreign trade again. President Hoover was officially a Republican, and the Republicans have been blamed for the Great Depression ever since. The stock market crash of 1929 probably was the catalyst for the Great Depression, but progressive policies by the Fed and ideas by both Hoover and FDR prolonged it. World War II pulled America out of the depression because we needed tanks, bombs, etc.

In recent years, America experienced a major recession which was blamed by the Democrats and the liberal media, on George Bush and the banks. And rightfully so to a certain extent. President Bush implemented new programs that any good liberal would be happy to claim. His education and drug programs added hundreds of billions of new debt to our country. The 2008 recession was in great part due to a crash in the real estate market. President Bush should have done something about this situation. However, the core problem goes back to President Clinton. If someone buys a home in America, there is about a 90% chance that their mortgage will be sold to Fannie Mae or Freddie Mac. These are government-sponsored enterprises. Their liabilities are guaranteed by the U.S. Government. They were started to be able to provide money to banks so that banks would have more money to loan and therefore more people would be able to buy homes. Fannie Mae was started by FDR in 1938 and the Freddie Mac came along in 1970. John Allison's book, "The Financial Crisis and the Free Market Cure" points out that President Clinton decided that more people needed to buy homes. He, therefore, pressured Fannie Mae and Freddie Mac and Allison shows "to make high-risk loans that were given priority over safety and soundness." For a long time, people were required to make 20% down payments, have good credit, and adhere to certain debt to income ratios in order to qualify for home loans. When these standards were relaxed, people with no down payment money and bad credit were able to get mortgages. There were plastic signs at street corners that said, $500 move in, bad credit ok. These people might have to pay higher interest rates, but few were turned down. Lenders saw the opportunity to make windfall profits, and after all, Fannie Mae and Freddie Mac had promised to buy the mortgages anyway. Home sales skyrocketed. Real estate agents couldn't keep enough homes in their inventory. Builders sprang up in every area of the country. Every business or occupation that had anything to do with new home sales was happy. Lenders were getting homes back when their owners were not able to make the payments, but the prices of homes were going up so fast that the re-possessed homes were worth more than what they had financed. That is, until it hit its peak. More and more people were not able to make their payments, and the market became saturated with homes. The price of homes began to plummet, and now the re-possessed homes were not worth what had been financed. AIG, had promised to insure or cover these mortgages and consequently lost billions. The government had to give AIG a bailout to keep them from closing their doors. The problem dominoed starting in 2007 through 2008. Homebuilders, lenders, real estate agents, and the associated businesses and contractors that had thrived now were in trouble. The housing market affects most of our economy directly and indirectly, and when it crashed so did our stock market and consequently so did our overall economy. Hundreds of thousands of people lost their job. President Clinton is never mentioned as having anything to do with the 2008 economic collapse. According to the mainstream media and the politicians and even the mainstream Republicans, it was George Bush and the banks.

We need more taxes according to liberal politicians. The wealthy can afford to pay more, and after all, if the average person is not one of those wealthy people then again, why should they care? Corporations need to pay more taxes. The corporate tax rate we currently have in America just gets passed on to the public. The price of new cars goes up substantially every year. The car companies pass along taxes, as well as the cost of new regulations that the politicians passed, for our benefit. Have any poor people ever given you a job? Bernard Marcus, the founder of Home Depot, that employs thousands, said raising taxes destroys jobs. Thomas Sowell wrote in his book, Intellectuals and Society, that intellectuals don't care about the results of their decisions as long as they are on the side of the angels. In other words, as mentioned earlier but bears repeating, as long as their cause seems just then the consequences of their actions are irrelevant. Plus, these decisions don't affect them. They send their children to private schools while they vote against school voucher programs where parents can choose which school they want to send their children to. What built America's economy to be the strongest and most opportunistic economy in the world was capitalism. Millions of people risk their lives to come to America because of the opportunities available to anyone who is willing to work and learn. Immigration has now slowed down from countries like China and India because at least a form of capitalism is being promoted there, and consequently more opportunities are available to people who before capitalism was embraced, were in poverty. The economies in these countries are improving rapidly, as a result. Politicians and entertainers frequently admonish successful people for being wealthy at the same time they are making millions. Hillary Clinton admonishes the wealthy though she and former President Bill Clinton own four mansions worth over $1 million each and President Clinton was ranked in the top ten richest Presidents with an estimated net worth of $55 million. Johnny Paycheck's song, "Take this Job and Shove it" was the anthem of people who resented success. In recent years, Democrat politicians supported the anti-Wall Street protests, though many of the wealthiest Congressmen (Democrats more so than Republicans) made a large part of their enormous wealth because of Wall Street. Goldman Sachs, one of the largest investment banks in the world makes huge contributions to the Democratic Party. John Allison stated in his book, The Financial Crisis and the Free Market Cure, that Goldman Sachs is the ultimate crony capitalist. He went on to say," Many Goldman Sachs alumni are in various high-level policy positions in Washington. Allison pointed out that Goldman is not the problem. Instead, the problem is that the politicians and bureaucrats who have this power. "If the U.S. Constitution was enforced, crony capitalism would not work because the politicians and bureaucrats would not have the authority to hand out favors to their friends." Immigrants coming to America excel frequently because they are willing to work longer hours and go above and beyond what is simply necessary. Proponents of bigger government and ever-increasing government programs, criticize over-achievers today. Remarks are made about these people not spending enough time with their family because of their greed. They are called brown-nosers if they work harder than the next person, they show up for work early, they volunteer for overtime, and therefore earn promotions. America has a history of people who seized the opportunities available to them and sometimes built very successful companies from nothing, regardless of their race or their starting position in life.

President Ronald Reagan believed that if large corporations were doing well, they would hire more people, invest in new products, which would again cause them to need more people. Some refer to this as trickle-down economics. I would just call it common sense. The theory is that, if large corporations are making more money and they feel comfortable about making more money in the future, they will hire more people, produce more products, and therefore supporting companies will hire more people and produce more products. Example; if a large home building corporation is doing well, they will require more lumber to build new homes, and therefore when the lumber company is doing well, then they will buy more logs from the company that harvests the trees, and therefore more loggers are employed. As more trees are harvested, then someone has a job to re-plant new trees. Then someone has a job to harvest seeds, so they can be replanted, and someone has a job to spray and nurture the new trees so more will grow, and so on and so on. The 20 years after President Reagan decreased taxes and implemented his trickle-down economics, American unemployment decreased almost to a level (below 5%) where there was essentially no unemployment. Consequently, large and small businesses were opening and thriving like never before. New home construction was up.

It's just common sense. If big companies are struggling or not making profits, how many new people are they going to hire? Nada. Zero. And, if you are working at one of these companies and hoping to get a promotion or a raise, what do you think the chances of that happening are? Slim and none. But just like Elvis, common sense has left the building!

Yet the Democratic Party insists that America needs more government, more regulations, more taxes even though the Carter administration had shown the folly in that strategy. Regulations are like a blockage in the arteries of this country. Small businesses are especially hard hit by onerous regulations, and they can't afford to pay the lobbyist to arrange a special exemption like large companies can. Richard Fisher the Dallas Fed president said the regulatory mountain "keeps building on itself and by continuing to do so its scaring job creation away." Currently, the Federal Regulatory Code has 160,000 pages. There were 3600 new federal regulations passed in 2013. This has become an out of control behemoth. Federal regulatory costs equal almost half of the federal budget. In May of 2014, U.S. News and World Report showed that almost 40% of U.S. jobs require a license issued by the government. Want to open a florist shop in Louisiana? It will cost you about $2,000, and will require taking an 80-hour course. Opening a restaurant in Los Angeles requires the approval of a dozen different agencies. Hotels are now required to have access to miniature horses as service animals! The Brookings Institute reported that more small businesses are now shutting down than starting up. Yes, we need some regulations but not the literally thousands that are passed each year. Plus, the regulations should be imposed by the states, not the Federal Government. The Constitution is very clear what the Federal Government can do and not do, and it states that anything other than what is spelled out is therefore left to the states. Some of these agencies are completely out of control. Such was the case in Texas in 2009. The Weekly Standard reported, Stephen Lipsky noticed a problem with his water well at his home near Dallas. He suspected a nearby natural gas well that range resources had built and fracked earlier that year. EPA testing showed traces of methane (well below the safe limits) in the water. Al Armendariz of the EPA slapped Range Resources with an endangering finding and remediation order. He stated, "We know they polluted that well." The EPA did not conduct elementary investigations before issuing the order. Range Resources took the case to court where it was discovered that the methane came from a natural source below the aquifer that supplied water to the well and that the natural gas well had nothing to do with the methane. The EPA claimed that the law didn't require them to prove or even allege any connection between Range Resources and the contamination. One of the founding fathers, James Madison stated, "It will be of little avail to the people if the laws are so voluminous that they cannot be read, or so incoherent that they cannot be understood." Most of the new laws or regulations that come out of Washington now have two or three thousand pages. In most cases, the House and Senate vote on them without really knowing what is in them. This needs to stop.

Breitbart reported that the Bureau of Land Management has the intent to seize 90,000 acres belonging to private landholders on the border of Texas and Oklahoma and turn it into federal land. Governor Abbott from Texas says that the BLM is ignoring the rule of law. However, the fourth branch of government, the Regulatory Branch, doesn't concern itself with things like the Constitution.

Art Laffer, President Reagan's economic adviser once said, "You can't keep milking the cow unless you feed her." In other words, businesses can't grow unless they are making money and they can't make money if taxes are too high or if there are too many regulations that inhibit them.

In 1993, Ann Richards, the Governor of Texas, attempted to pass a law that would require all small businesses to provide health insurance for their employees. Her law failed to pass. However, there was a compromise, health insurers would be required to issue coverage for the small businesses that chose to provide it, on a guaranteed issue basis. The result? Health insurance premiums went through the roof and consequently many small businesses that were providing employee coverage had to drop it because of the expense. The real problems with health insurance will be addressed later.

Today the Fed is manipulating the economy by printing money and telling banks to loan this money out to stimulate the economy. These banks are loaning this money to large institutional investors who are investing it into the market. This huge influx of capital has been artificially inflating the market since President Obama took office. As Obama's second term started on its last two years, the Fed announced it would be tapering off how much money they were infusing into the economy. Because the market is artificially inflated there is a big risk of a major correction on the horizon. The market was artificially inflated in 1999 and again in 2007 which resulted in 40% losses to peoples 401ks and IRAs in many cases.

Our government is out of control when it comes to spending. The government debt has gone up over 200% under President George W Bush and President Barack Obama. What will happen when the countries that we owe want their money, and we can't pay?

Here are some other ways the government gets control of American's hard earned money.

Gasoline tax. The federal tax on Gasoline is 18.4 cents per gallon, and the state tax is much higher. It averages about .31 but is over .50 per gallon in California. Recently when the price of oil went down, Democrats and Republicans, both commented that this would be a good time to raise the gasoline tax. Most Americans would probably not have a problem with this tax if it all went to rebuilding our roads and such, but too many of our tax dollars are directed to programs that have nothing to do with what they were intended. In an article from CNN Money, Grover Norquist, the head of Americans for Tax Reform stated, "Much money is siphoned off to pay union workers or to build bike paths... not roads." According to the Department of Transportation, approximately 15% of these federal funds go toward mass transit and other things not road related.

Then, howeve,r the government subsidizes refineries that mix ethanol with gasoline. That strategy was supposed to help America become less dependent on foreign oil according to President Carter who started it. It has had no impact on foreign dependency but has caused the price of corn to go up not just in America but around the world. Ethanol burns less efficient than gasoline resulting in less mileage per gallon. Who does the ethanol that is put in gasoline help? It helps the corporate farmers who get higher prices for their corn, and it helps the politician who represents the corporate farmers. This bill was called the Volumetric Ethanol Excise tax credit. Originally when Jimmy carter started this program, it was a tax exemption.

George W. Bush changed it to a tax credit in 2004. Ethanol blenders are credited .45 per gallon. Mexico depends heavily on corn for food, and there have been numerous protests in Mexico as our so-called environmental programs that promote ethanol have driven up their food costs.

The sugar subsidy program is another example of government waste of your money. According to the Washington Post on November 25, 2013, The U.S. Department of Agriculture lost $280 million dollars on their sugar subsidy program due to Mexico driving down the price of sugar. Jimmy Carter loved big government. During his tenure inflation rates skyrocketed causing interest rates to do the same. If someone wanted to buy a home and finance it during the Carter years, they might have to pay 18% interest on that loan. Government can't fix our problems, they are the problem.

 Airline tax. Cigarette tax. Liquor tax, also called sin taxes, property and school tax, state tax, sales tax, and most highways are becoming toll roads which is another tax. When you register your car that is a tax. Buy a fishing license? Yes, that's a tax. When high net worth people leave money to their heirs, that is called estate taxes (most call it the death tax). Have you been on vacation or stayed in a hotel for business? The hotel tax in some cities is ridiculous. If you are self-employed or own a small business in some states, you must pay a franchise tax. Truckers pay highway access fees on top of the fees they pay on diesel. Next month look at your phone bill and see all the different taxes for who knows what. We don't pay taxes when we buy food at the grocery store, but we do pay taxes on our food when we eat out, and most families eat out at least once per week. There are probably hundreds of additional taxes not mentioned, but the bottom line is taxes are out of control. The Federal Government has made the tax code so confusing hardly anyone comes up with the same answers. The Federal Tax code now has over 3 million words. Highways, schools, the post office, and the military are necessary for us. But should we really be paying taxes, so the government can pay for a study on why Chinese prostitutes have alcohol problems? Should we really be paying taxes, so our government can loan money to companies like China Airlines? Because maybe China Airlines will promise to buy Boeing planes? This is done through the "Export/Import Bank."

Now some states are proposing a new payroll tax to provide a state-run retirement plan. Why does anyone need to be responsible? Why shouldn't they spend every dime they get their hands on. After all, the government will take care of them. Again, that "Patron" mentality.

A typical family with a combined income of $60,000 per year will pay at least 30% of their income in various taxes. Huffington Post reported that the average person works until April 12th each year just to pay their Federal Income Tax. And now, Bernie Sanders, a democratic/socialist candidate for president, wants to add another $19 trillion to the tax bill. Winston Churchill once said, "We contend that for a nation to try to tax itself into prosperity is like a man standing in a bucket and trying to lift himself up by the handle."

So where does all this revenue go? According to justfacts.com:

1. Defense spending used to be approximately 40% of federal spending. Now it makes up only 21%, and that number is going down. Our Navy and Air Force are at smaller levels than they have been in fifty years. Even North Korea has more ships than

our Navy. Our veterans struggle to get medical help in the VA hospitals.

2. Social programs make up over 60% of federal spending. This includes Social Security, healthcare, food stamps, education, housing, grants for entertainment and arts. This area has shown a steady increase in spending since 1992. Often discretionary spending bills will be attached, piggybacked, or earmarked to another bill that almost everyone is already in favor of. For instance, a highway bill. It's usually pretty easy to convince people to support a bill to improve the highways in America. But then politicians will do something like attach a bill to fund a study about why lesbians are obese! That's a real study by the way. But no one objects because they would be accused of objecting to the highway bill. So how does this affect the average American? There are approximately 322,000,000 people in the U.S. Shortly after Obama took office, the government loaned $500,000,000 to a company called Solyndra that shortly after declared bankruptcy and closed its doors. What if the government would have made that money available to anyone who wanted to get off welfare to use for education or to start a small business. But then those people wouldn't be dependent on the government, would they? The government gives millions of dollars each year to Egypt. Put that money back into the coffers and most of the middle class wouldn't have to pay any income taxes.

3. General government and debt services are at 14%. This includes the cost to run the executive and legislative branches of the government plus the IRS and the interest owed on the federal debt. A partial list of executive transportation costs

show the past administration enjoyed spending your tax dollars. The Obamas visited South Africa and Hawaii in 2013. The flight cost alone for these two trips was over $15 million dollars. The Washington Post reported that the total cost for the African trip was around $100 million. President Obama attended several fundraisers for Democrat candidates. One of which was to California costing $1,176,120. At 13, Malia Obama spent her spring break in Mexico which required 25 Secret Service agents to accompany her. And one golf and family vacation for the Obamas in 2015 cost $3,115,688. Total travel costs for the Obamas has been $70,880,035. In many cases, Judicial Watch had to sue to get this information.

4. Economic affairs 4%. This includes things like the Department of Agriculture (where we pay farmers not to grow products), the Department of Energy (where we loan hundreds of millions of dollars to solar energy companies that then file bankruptcy), space (NASA), and other worthwhile economic issues and endeavors. In 1977, the Department of Energy was formed to supposedly lessen America's dependence on buying oil from the Middle East. Today the Department of Energy employs approximately 16,000 people and has an annual budget of approximately $24 billion dollars, and we are still dependent on foreign oil. Then, there's some overlap. Foreign Affairs may fall into several categories. America gives billions to a whole list of countries, many who hate us. Why is the government giving billions to these countries when America is so far in debt? Here is a partial list of the billions paid out.

Hamas (Most Americans recognize as a terrorist organization) $351 Million

Libya $1.45 Billion

Egypt $397 million

Mexico $622 Million

Russia $380 Million

Haiti $1.4 Billion

Jordan $463 Million

Kenya $816 Million

Sudan $870 Million

Nigeria $456 Million

Uganda $451 Million

Congo $359 Million

Ethiopia $981 Million

Pakistan $2 Billion

South Africa $566 Million

Senegal $698 million

Mozambique $404 Million

Zambia $331 million

Kazakhstan $304 Million

Iraq $1.08 Billion

Tanzania $554 Million

The U.S. even gives $65 Million a year to China which has the second largest economy in the world!

Huffington Post reported on 8-30-2012 that America gives approximately 50 billion dollars in foreign aid each year. "The world's top donor, by far."

Millions of American tax dollars are being spent to rebuild mosques and to pay for internet service in the Middle East with the rationale from the State Department, that they are trying to build relationships with Islamic leaders. This internet service helps these radicals to spew their violent rhetoric and helps them to recruit more weak-minded people to their cause. Many of these mosques are in areas that support radical Islamic terrorists.

To put this in plain English, the government is taking in somewhere over 2 trillion dollars, but they are spending almost 4 trillion dollars. The government is taking money from American citizens and giving it to other countries. This is money that reduces the lifestyle of Americans. This is money that Americans could use to send their kids to college. This is money that could be set aside for people's retirement. The U.S. Government is sending millions of dollars to other countries to improve their lifestyle, so their kids can go to college, and so they can have a better retirement, and in many cases so their politicians can live extravagant lifestyles. In reality, most of this money does not go to the people in these countries. The other crazy part of this story is that many of these countries hate the U.S. Last week. Russian nuclear submarines were patrolling close to where our internet cables cross the ocean. In recent months, Russian bombers capable of carrying nuclear weapons have been piercing U.S. airspace to test the reaction of the U.S.

military, yet Russia gets foreign aid from America! China has recently built man-made islands in the South China Sea with military airstrips. This area has historically been claimed by China, Vietnam, Taiwan, the Philippines, and Malaysia, and the U.S. has kept the peace between all of the claimants. China has decided to boot everyone else out and has told the U.S. NAVY to get out of the area. The U.S. has borrowed over 1 trillion dollars from China, and yet again the U.S. gives China foreign aid. It's absurd. The U.S. borrows money and then gives it away. Or sometimes, just gives away assets because it seems like the nice thing to do. In 1881, France attempted to build a canal across Panama to make it easier to get from the Atlantic Ocean to the Pacific Ocean or vice versa. France gave up and sold the area to the U.S. in 1904. Teddy Roosevelt then proceeded to intercede and help Panama become independent from Columbia. A treaty was written with Panama to give the U.S. basically a forever lease. The cost to build the Panama Canal in today's dollars would be over 14 billion dollars. No other country was able to construct this engineering marvel. This canal proved to be an extremely strategic asset to the U.S. during World War II helping with not only commerce but also the defense of America. A military base was constructed to defend the canal and until 1999 this base employed over 18,000 Panamanians. In 1977, President Jimmy Carter due to student protests in Panama, signed a treaty to simply give the Panama Canal back to Panama. The 18,000 Panamanians lost their job at the U.S. base, consequently. America did not get compensated for the canal. America did not get any agreements that in case of hostilities that America would still retain some strategic control. The only agreement Jimmy Carter got out of this was that the Panamanians said the canal will always be neutral. Today a Chinese company controls both ends of the canal. President

Carter just gave it away. One example after another of U.S. politicians giving away U.S. money or U.S. assets away to other countries. What do these politicians receive in return? Libya is an oil-rich country. Why is the U.S. giving them over $1 billion per year? Mexico's people may live like a 3rd world country, but Mexico is rich in minerals and resources. Why did the U.S. give Mexico $622 million last year? The U.S. gave $1.4 billion to Haiti. Five years after a devastating earthquake, Haiti still has over 200,000 people living in tents! Where did that money go? Are you mad yet?

Several of the countries that the U.S. gives foreign aid to are oil-rich countries just like Libya. Pakistan is number 26 in the world for GDP. They are rich in minerals and coal. They have a very successful manufacturing sector. They aren't broke. But guess who is broke. The United States of America is broke. Yes, the United States of America is broke. The U.S. owes numerous foreign countries currently right at 22 trillion dollars. What happens when these countries want their money? Today, the U.S. dollar is used as the currency of the world. All oil is bought with U.S. dollars. It doesn't matter if Russia is buying oil from Iran or Saudia Arabia, they buy that oil with U.S. dollars. There are some countries referred to as BRIC nations (Brazil, Russia, India, China) that want to change that. If the U.S. dollar loses its hold as the global currency the value of the U.S. dollar will become worthless. After all, the U.S. dollar is only backed by the ability to pay its debts, and if America can't pay her debts, then the dollar will be worth absolutely nothing. If someone has money in the bank or maybe a 401k, it will become like monopoly money overnight. Each year the Congress votes to spend more money. This is like a scene in a movie where a naval officer was asked, "That is a bad idea. Is this the best idea you have?" and the officer responded, "This is the best bad idea we have, sir." They pass budgets like it's the best bad idea they have. They must have missed the class where they were supposed to have learned how to balance their checkbook. Recently, the administration discovered that they had overpaid Social Security benefits, between the years 2008-2013, by $128.3 million. In an audit, the Inspector General discovered that our inept government spent 323 million dollars to recover that $128.3 million. Is it any wonder why America is so much in debt? Yet if someone stands up and says this must stop, then politicians threaten to shut down the government, and our congress people and senators back down and compromise so they won't lose any votes back home. Congress just recently passed a budget and wanted Americans to believe it was positive because it could have been worse. This budget gave President Obama a blank checkbook. He could spend anything he wanted, and it was spun as a big help to the economy. So again, they said they raised the deficit less than expected! Why does America have a deficit? Why is the most successful country in history borrowing money from anyone? When someone makes $40,000 per year they probably shouldn't buy a Ferrari? They should buy what fits into their budget. Why can't the government operate the same way? Why haven't the politicians pursued some of the flat tax ideas or tried to reform or simplify the tax system? Because politicians want to get re-elected, so they make promises. The politicians like all of the loopholes that are in the current tax system. They make promises to the big corporations to exempt them from some of the taxes and then the big corporations donate millions to their campaigns. Promises and more promises. Now, there are some presidential candidates promising even more. Free college, free healthcare, and more, and more, and more. Understand, the government does not make money. They spend money that Americans make, and they are spending more money than the American people are capable of making. Between what is owed to other countries and what the government owes us in Social Security and Medicare/Medicaid benefits, etc., If they took every dollar from all the rich people in the U.S., every dollar, it wouldn't come close to paying the bill. But they will promise more to get people's vote because, quite honestly, they just don't think the American people are smart enough to realize what is happening.

So, why are most people so complacent about these money issues? Again it's because of manipulation. See, money isn't real to many Americans today. When they talk about $22 trillion dollars. What does that mean? Why do casinos use poker chips instead of cash? Watch someone at a blackjack table go from being $40,000 ahead to giving it all back to the casino. If there were cash or the title to a car on the table would that person be as willing to donate to the casino as they are when they are just using colored plastic chips? Probably not. Now, the casinos have become smarter when it comes to slot machines. They don't use real money, just credits. And one of the biggest manipulations is the penny slots. It's just a penny, right? Now it is common to have to bet 25 to 50 pennies to win a decent jackpot, but the perception is that a penny slot won't lose as much as a quarter slot. Credit works in a similar way. Credit used to be difficult to obtain. Not anymore. Commercials on television state no credit check. Many commercials tout "no payments till next year." Almost anyone can get a credit card today. Then when their balance reaches $20,000 they just pay the minimum balance. And when they can't even pay that anymore, they go to a service that negotiates a payment program for them. Some people hardly carry cash anymore. Just charge it! Our government operates the same way, but when the incredible amount of debt is discussed, it doesn't register with the average person. Almost 22 trillion dollars. How much is a trillion dollars? A trillion seconds ago was 33,000 years. What is a few billion here and there? The House of Representatives just passed a trillion dollar spending bill. That means that every man, woman, and child in America just went into debt another $3,000. With the other $22 trillion that means that everyone owes $60,000, but because 50% of Americans don't pay any federal income taxes, the number for most taxpayers is much higher than that. How does that affect someone? The average American works for taxes through April of each year! This debt will affect the future ability to fund Social Security and Medicare. It will affect the ability to defend America, if necessary. It will affect the ability to build and repair highways. Politicians vote to spend these insane amounts of money with no more concern than that person at the blackjack table because it's not real money. It is just a trillion dollars worth of plastic poker chips. That's the governments problem, right? Very few people really got upset when they heard that another trillion was being spent even though most people probably would have disagreed with what a lot of that trillion was spent on. See, reality is that most Americans would like to get upset, but this has happened so many times that they are now calloused or cynical and have decided that they can't do anything about it. Although most know this system is broke, for the most part, most have indoor plumbing, even people considered below the poverty line have color televisions, microwave ovens, and cell phones. When this debt substantially affects the average American's daily living, then people will stand up and demand that something must be done.

The news talks about the fluctuating value of the U.S. dollar, but very few people pay much attention. Nations increase the value or decrease the value of their currency sometime to give them a competitive advantage with importing and exporting. Today there are commercials every day from people who believe that it is inevitable that the value of the U.S. dollar will crash in the near future. If this happens, what will happen to people's savings or their 401k? After World War II the U.S. dollar became the global reserve for the world. The dollar was backed by the gold reserves of the U.S. After the Vietnam War, LBJ had spent so much money that there was not enough gold in the U.S. reserves to back up the dollar. In 1971 Richard Nixon, therefore, separated the dollar from gold in order to keep from paying out all the U.S.. gold to cover the debt.

5. Public order and safety 2%. The U.S. spends more on things like solar energy than border security and public safety. This area includes law enforcement, the federal courts, federal prisons and the border patrol and immigration service. Of course, there is no problem there. Terrorists pouring over our porous borders shouldn't concern Americans, should it? Once again, control and votes are the dominant motivators for this manipulation. Allowing immigrants to cross the border seemingly unchallenged sometimes, is presented to Americans as a humanitarian thing to do. The legalization by President Obama's executive action of these illegals was intended to increase the Democratic voting base. As soon as he signed this order, the conversation began about allowing these so-called guest workers to vote.

Where is all this increased spending coming from? In 2009 and 2010 between the House of Representatives and the U.S. Senate, 176 bills were presented to reduce spending, however 2,480 bills were presented that would increase spending. Who is pushing all this spending? As mentioned before, if someone wants to build a solar power plant or a new dam in their area, they hire a lobbyist to persuade the Representatives or senators to vote for their project. Then they convince those members of Congress to attach their project (called earmarks) to another project that almost everyone is already in favor of, or that has an emotional value, i.e. something that anyone that would vote against it would certainly be un-American or heartless. Therefore, to vote against their project would be to vote against the overwhelmingly popular project. It's a game. Hey, if you vote for my new dam, I will vote for your solar energy plant. President Calvin Coolidge was one of the only presidents that balanced the budget in America. He stated, "I want the people of America to be able to work less for the government and more for themselves. I want them to have the rewards of their own industry. This is the chief meaning of freedom." There needs to be some of that thinking today.

Lobbyists and special interest advocates proliferate Washington D.C. today. The median income for a starting lobbyist, according to salary.com, is $112,000. Many of these jobs pay much more depending on the area and the political ties and experience of the lobbyist.

What is a lobbyist? Basically, a professional persuader that tries to convince a legislator to vote a certain way or to approve of an allotment of money for their cause.

Nothing but old rich white guys

That's the perception of the Republican party, or at least the perception that is fed to the public. The media feeds the public much like the Pablum previous generations were fed as babies. Younger people won't know what Pablum is, but basically, it means what babies were spoon fed that was supposed to be good for them. They ate it because they didn't know any better. It tastes like paste. What is referred to as the mainstream media, which is made up of the main three network television stations plus many of the main newspapers and magazines, has been in bed with the Democratic party for a long time. They tell the very carefully selected stories or part of stories they want the public to hear. Reporters and so-called journalists have promoted liberal politicians over the years, but the level of prejudice the last few years has become ridiculous. The mainstream media tends to paint Republicans as, 1. Rich old white men, 2. They don't care about the poor, 3. They are predominantly racists, 4. They like to go to war every chance they get. 5. They want dirty water and dirty air and making money is more important than caring about the environment. 6. They want to keep women barefoot and pregnant.

 There are probably some more stereotypes, but let's look at these.

1. The average age of a Republican voter is 50. The average democrat voter is 47. The average personal income of Republicans in 2010 was $30,275, and the average for Democrats was slightly higher coming in at $36,327. Out of the top 10 richest congressmen, 7 are Democrats. Eight out of ten of the wealthiest districts in the U.S. are Democrat strongholds. In the last 100 years, four out of the top five of the richest presidents were Democrats. President Clinton's wealth is currently estimated now at over 100 million dollars. JFK in today's dollars would have been worth 1 billion dollars. One truth is that the Republican party is definitely a mostly white party. Why? Look at the previous chapter.

2.   In 2011, the IRS reported that the predominantly red states, states that vote Republican, gave more to charities, gave blood, and volunteered more often than blue states by a margin of 2/1. Conservative Christians fund and actively participate in mission trips all over the world more than any other organization. An organization called the Texas Baptist Men respond to national and international emergencies in many cases much better than FEMA. When a tornado struck Moore Oklahoma last year, thousands of residents lost their entire home. While many of these residents were asking and waiting for the Federal Government to help, the Texas Baptist Men had already started rebuilding their homes. In 2004, there was a massive earthquake in the Indian Ocean which caused a Tsunami that killed 230,000 people in Indonesia, Sri Lanka and Thailand. The

U.S. Government gave 1 billion dollars but nongovernmental agencies and private donations added up to over 1.8 billion dollars. Catholic Relief Services gave 190 million dollars. Just as a comparison to show how generous America is, China gave $67 million, and Russia gave $2 million to this disaster. The Democrats believe that the government should take care of the poor rather than churches or charities. In an ABC News article on April 26, 2013, they stated that George W. Bush did more for Africa than any other president.

3. Abraham Lincoln was considered by many to be one of our best Presidents. He fought and won a civil war that ended slavery in our country. Slavery, however, was not the only reason for the Civil War. President Lincoln didn't free the slaves in the north until 1862, a year after the war started. Stopping slavery was a great thing that probably wouldn't have happened for a long time had the civil war not happened. The slaves in America were owned mostly by the southern aristocracy, which by the way were predominantly Democrats! Less than 2% of Americans owned slaves. There were also approximately 3,500 Black slave owners, and in fact, the first official slave owner in America was Black. His name was Anthony Johnson. In 1654, Anthony Johnson went to court and sued for ownership of an indentured servant. There were also over 100,000 Irish slaves in America. I wonder why that wasn't in our history books? King James II sold 30,000 Irish slaves to the new world starting in 1625. In the 1650s, 52,000 Irish slaves went to Jamaica, Barbados, and Antigua but many were also sent to Virginia. The English killed hundreds of thousands of Irish and sold hundreds of thousands more into slavery. Thousands of Irish children from 10-14 years old were taken from their parents and sold as slaves. This left thousands of Irish women who were sold and sometimes bred to African slaves because of the light colored children that

resulted. In the 16th and 17th centuries, there were over 1 million White European slaves stolen and taken to the Barbary Coast area of Africa by the same Arab slave traders who sold Africans to Europe and the west. The European slaves were taken by Barbary pirates from Morocco, Tunisia, and Libya and by raids from Italy all the way to the Netherlands. The Barbary slave trade ended when the U.S.A. defeated these pirates when Thomas Jefferson decided he had enough and he sent a new military group started just for that purpose, called the United States Marines. Numerous Native American tribes owned Black slaves but also slaves from other tribes. The Jewish people were held in slavery by Egypt for 400 years, and Rome took slaves literally from every country in the European, Asian, and African continents. The Japanese had slaves. The Chinese had slaves. The sad truth is, that slavery was part of almost every country or civilizations history for over 2,000 years.

 Abraham Lincoln, who is credited with ending slavery, was a Republican. In fact, the Republican party was started by anti-slavery activists in 1854. In 1862, Abraham Lincoln signed the bill to abolish slavery. The 13th Amendment that abolished slavery was approved by 99% of Republicans. Slavery was stopped by a bunch of White Republicans. At least in America. Slavery still exists in some Arab countries today. Most Democrats were against the bill, and in fact, 83% voted against it. May 10th, 1866, the 14th Amendment was passed. This amendment gave former slaves citizenship. 100% of Democrats voted against it.

Over 5 million slaves were stolen from Africa and sold into slavery of which less than 10% came to America. The over whelming majority of African slaves sent to the new world from the 1500s through the 1800s were sent to the Caribbean and South America. Millions of African slaves were sent to South

America. Approximately 388,000 African slaves were sent to America during that same time frame. Slavery again has been part of every civilization in human history, but it was a group of mostly White Republicans in America that put an end to it. In fact, over 300,000 mostly White men died to end this plague. Only then did other countries begin to end slavery. After the Civil War many of the southern Democrats, although defeated, weren't going to give up their racial ideals just yet. After the war, a group of southern Democrats, started a new para-military group, referring to themselves as the Klu Klux Klan, continued to wage a silent war against anyone who wasn't a White protestant. This group murdered numerous black and White Republicans. On September 28th, 1868, a KKK mob murdered over 399 Black Republicans in Opelousas, Louisiana. Dr. Eric Foner, a liberal historian, wrote in his book, A Short History of Reconstruction, "That the Klan was a military force serving the interests of the Democratic Party, the planter class, and all those who desired the restoration of White Supremacy. It aimed to destroy the Republican Party infrastructure, undermine the Reconstruction state, reestablish control of the Black labor force and restore racial subordination in every aspect of Southern life."

In 1871, Republicans passed the anti-Klu Klux Klan Act, outlawing Democratic terrorists groups. The first KKK group was founded in 1865 in Pulaski Tennessee by Democrats. It didn't matter if someone was Black or Jewish or even Catholic. The Klan didn't like any of them. The Klan was re-energized in 1915 after a Pro- Klan motion picture called "The Birth of a Nation" which was a favorite of President Woodrow Wilson. A distinctive member of the Klan was Senator Robert Byrd (Democrat), who was a KKK recruiter and was at one time unanimously elected to be the exalted cyclops, which is the top officer in his Klan unit, stated that the Klan was effective in promoting traditional American values. Senator Byrd wrote in a letter to Senator Theodore Bilbo in 1946, "I shall never fight in the armed forces with a Negro by my side…rather I should die a thousand times, and see Old Glory trampled in the dirt never to rise again than to see this beloved land of ours become degraded by race mongrels, a throwback to the blackest specimen from the wilds." Senator Byrd said that Martin Luther King Jr. was a troublemaker, and that he liked to start trouble but then run away like a coward. By the way, Senator Barack Obama wrote a letter in support of Senator Byrd. Even Harry Truman (Democrat) wore the white hood for a short time and only quit because of the way the Klan treated Catholics. From 1869 to 1935, every Black elected to Congress was a Republican. At the 1924 Democratic convention, 40,000 Klan members attended. The Democratic delegates debated and fought over the platform but in the end, the Klan won. The Klan was in favor of violence and intimidation against Blacks and Catholics. The final vote was 546 for and 542 against. Even when the facts are shown, there are still individuals like Congressman Elijah Cummings who recently stated that Democrats were responsible for Blacks getting the right to vote. Incidentally, there wasn't one Democratwho voted in favor of the 15th Amendment which gave Black people the right to vote.

The only states that voted Democrat in the 1924 presidential election were the 11 southern Democratic states. After the Civil War, the Democrats gradually regained power in the southern legislatures and over the years legislated the Jim Crow laws, segregating Blacks from Whites. In 1948, southern Democrats called the "Dixiecrats" tried to keep the Jim Crowe laws alive. In the 1950s, there were "colored" restrooms and water fountains. I grew up in the south, but I lived much of the time on Air Force bases, and our Black next-door neighbors were frequently at our house for dinner. No one told us we were supposed to not like each other.

 Woodrow Wilson (Democrat) was an extreme racist. He thought the KKK was a great organization. He terminated all Blacks from posts in his administration as soon as he took office, and also segregated the military. When he was the president of Princeton, he rejected Blacks applications because he considered them to be ignorant and inferior. Although FDR (Democrat) said he wanted to help blacks improve their situation, he banned Black American newspapers from the military because he thought they were communist. He appointed Hugo Black, a KKK member to the Supreme Court. His Public Works Administration built segregated housing and gave contractors special deals to build in those areas which has helped to keep those areas segregated today. He carried all the southern states when he was elected where Blacks had no hope for civil rights or the possibility to vote. In 1941, FDR appointed Senator Jimmy Byrnes to the Supreme Court. Byrnes was instrumental in stopping anti-lynching laws from being passed because he said lynching was necessary to keep Negros in check in the south. Harry Truman also named Jimmy Byrnes his secretary of state. In the 1936 summer Olympics in Berlin Germany, Jesse Owens won four Gold medals. He remarked that Hitler didn't snub him but that he never heard a word from his president (FDR) when he returned to America. In 1958, Dwight Eisenhower (Republican) established a permanent Civil Rights Commission which had been previously rejected by former presidents including FDR.

March 12th, 1956, 97 congressmen condemned the Supreme Court decision in Brown vs. Board of Education. This case ended segregation in public schools. President Dwight Eisenhower proposed a civil rights act in 1957 but the Democratic led Senate, run by LBJ fought against it. President Eisenhower was the first president since reconstruction to sign a civil rights act, and the first president since reconstruction to invite Black leaders to the White House. The idea that Blacks almost always vote Democrat is mostly a new phenomenon. Martin Luther King was a Republican. Although his son, Martin Luther King Jr. would not commit to either party he did vote for Dwight Eisenhower. He worked with President Nixon on civil rights because he couldn't get any help from the Democrats. Dr. Alveda King, Martin Luther King Jr.'s niece, stated that her grandfather, Martin Luther King was a Republican and his son, her uncle, Martin Luther King Jr she believed was also a Republican. There is a lot of people that don't believe that to be true. Most people don't know that the Republicans started the NAACP and that the first Black president of the NAACP was James Johnson, a Republican. The man referred to as the father of Affirmative Action, Art Fletcher, who coined the saying, "A mind is a terrible thing to waste." and who was also the president of the United Negro College Fund, was a Republican. Few know that Republicans started the Historically Black Colleges and Universities (HBCU's).

President Bill Clinton, without Congressional approval, sent 20,000 US troops to Bosnia but refused to send troops or weapons to stop the massacre of Rwandans in 1994. For generations, the two dominant tribes, (Hutus and Tutsis) in Rwanda had fought and struggled for dominance of their country, and when the President who was Hutu was killed by a rocket fired at his plane, the Hutus blamed the Tutsis and decided they should be exterminated. During the next 100 days, members of the Hutu tribe went door to door executing Tutsi tribe members. If these people had money to pay, they were given the opportunity to be shot otherwise if they couldn't pay for bullets they were either bludgeoned to death or killed with a machete. During this 100-day genocide, the Tutsis repeatedly asked President Clinton for weapons, so they could defend themselves, but he declined saying he didn't want to get involved in their civil war. Why was he agreeable to be involved in Bosnias civil war but not Rwanda. Somewhere between 800,000 and 1 million Tutsis were executed in those 100 days. Because there were more voters in America sympathetic to what was going on in Bosnia than the number of voters that were interested in Rwanda?

When Eisenhower proposed his civil right bill in 1957, overwhelmingly, Republicans voted for (90%) and 47% of Democrats voted against it, including Lyndon Johnson. LBJ biographer Robert Caro noted about Johnson, "Had never supported civil rights legislation, including anti-lynching legislation." On June 11th, 1963, President Kennedy met with Republican leaders to discuss civil rights and two days later a Republican, Everett Dirksen, introduced the bill. Al Gore Sr., the father of former Vice President Al Gore, led a filibuster to try and defeat the civil rights act proposed by Dirksen. Forty percent of Democrats voted against the act. Democratic Senator Richard Russell from Georgia, said, "We will resist to the bitter end any measure or any movement which would have a tendency to bring about social equality and intermingling and amalgamation of the races in our states." The Republicans voted in favor by 82% in the House and 96% in the Senate. Robert Kessler's, Inside the White House, reported that LBJs treatment of Blacks was appalling. Behind closed doors, LBJ said, "These Negros, they're getting pretty uppity these days. That's a problem for us, since they got something now they never had before. The political pull to back up their uppityness. Now, we've got to do something about this. We've got to give them a little something. Just enough to quiet them down, but not enough to make a difference. If we don't move at all, their allies will line up against us. And there'll be no way to stop them. It'll be Reconstruction all over again."

The Voting Rights Act of 1965, which has been in the news frequently during the last two elections, giving the right to vote for all was approved by 100%of Republicans and 0% of Democrats. The Voting Rights Act was proposed and championed by Everett Dirksen, a Republican. One of the most outspoken politicians against Blacks, segregation, and civil rights, was George Wallace, a Democrat. Frank Johnson, a Republican federal judge, is who ruled in favor of Rosa Parks. President Clinton has acclaimed William Fulbright as a great man and referred to him as his mentor. In fact, Senator Fulbright along with 100 other Senators and Congressmen (87 were Democrats) voted against the Civil Rights Act and the Voting Rights Act in 1964 and 1965. He also filibustered against the Civil Rights Act in 1957. Fulbright signed what was referred to as the southern manifesto which was a declaration that was against racial integration of public places. There were 101 politicians who signed this manifesto, 99 were Democrats. We are told that Republicans are racists, repeatedly by the mainstream media. This manipulation has gone so far that a memorial plaque on Northern Illinois University listed Abraham Lincoln as a Democrat. History shows us which party was racial, but people must open their eyes and quit blindly listening to any media outlets. These media outlets talk about White privilege. The truth according to the U.S. Census Bureau is that Whites rank 16th in average income in America. Indian Americans average approximately $40,000 per year more in average income than Whites. Nigerian Americans, Syrian Americans, and Egyptian Americans all show higher average income than Whites. Today we have some crusaders like Jesse Jackson, Al Sharpton, and Louis Farrakhan, who frequently lead racial protests. Think about it, if they ever admitted that most people in America don't care about the color of a man's skin, they would be out of a job. Booker T. Washington, a Black author, educator, and adviser to U.S. presidents, remarked, "There is a certain class of race-problem solvers who don't want the patient to get well, because as long as the disease holds out they have not only an easy means of making a living but also an easy medium through which to make themselves prominent before the public." Most believe Jesse Jackson coined the term, "African-American." John Wayne once gave a speech where he remarked that a hyphen fans the flames of racial hatred faster than almost anything. In an interview with Mike Wallace, Morgan Freeman, a great actor, stated, "I would like to be known as Morgan Freeman, not a Black man." It's a small group of people and the media that keep racism alive. Terms such as African-American or Latino or Hispanic, keep groups of people or voting blocks, divided. Most Whites in America want the Black/White issue to go away, but the dividers won't let it. This is part of a game plan that will be discussed later. It's not just a Black and White issue. Native Americans have also been led to believe these same myths, yet it was Calvin Coolidge, a Republican President and a Republican Congress who passed the bill making Native Americans, American citizens. The media stated several times in the last Presidential election that if Barack Obama wasn't elected it would be because of racism. Wake up America, 70% of President Obama's votes were Whites. So really, which party has been historically more racist

and why? If America is such a racist country, why have there been more Africans immigrate here voluntarily than all the slaves who were brought here. As stated above, 79% of Planned Parenthood clinics are in minority neighborhoods. Why are the Democrats so much in favor of these clinics? The truth is that, Democrats held Blacks down for 150 years until it was good for their game plan to start acting like they are supporting them. It is an act. It is all about controlling their votes.
Look at people's actions, not what they say.

4. Republicans are war mongers. In the 60s, Republicans were referred to as Hawks and the Democrats as Doves. But which politicians were really responsible for the wars that America has been involved with? The Civil War was started by southern Democrats because they wanted to stop Abraham Lincoln and his abolitionists from telling the states that they could not own slaves. 625,000 died in the Civil War. The United States entered World War I led by Woodrow Wilson, a Democrat and 116,516 Americans died. FDR took us into World War II, also a Democrat and 405,399 Americans lost their lives. Harry Truman was the President when we went to war with Korea, and by the way, he was a Democrat. 36,516 Americans died, as a result of the Korean War. And as was mentioned in an earlier chapter, LBJ (Democrat) wanted to have his own war. Although it was referred to as the Vietnam conflict, over 58,000 American soldiers lost their lives. Gerald Ford ended the Vietnam conflict, and he was a Republican. In the past 100 years, only George H.W. Bush, and then George W. Bush, were the only Republican Presidentswho have taken America to war. Since 2001, approximately 6,000 Americans have died in Iraq and Afghanistan. In 1898, the only other Republican to take America

to war was President McKinley who took America to war with Spain which lasted six months.

Ronald Reagan believed in having the strongest military in the world, and therefore, we will never have to go to war. Bullies pick on the weak not the strong.

5. Republicans want dirty air and dirty water
    This must be true because the Republicans believe the EPA is out of control and that there are entirely too many regulations which stifle businesses. Here is a big surprise for you. Richard Nixon started the EPA with an executive action on December 2nd, 1970, and by the way, Nixon was a Republican. Quickly, however, this agency became too powerful. Rachel Carson wrote a book called Silent Spring, about DDT back in the 60s claiming that children were getting cancer because of DDT and, just like global warming, even though there were no facts to back up her theory, the manipulators with the EPA decided to shut down the use of DDT. For the younger people who might be reading this, DDT was an insecticide that was extremely effective in controlling mosquitos. Malaria has always been a deadly problem especially in Africa, but the Africans were able to substantially reduce the amount of deaths related to malaria by using DDT. Malaria was well on its way to being eradicated in Africa. In March 1960, the Supreme Court ruled that there was no credible evidence that DDT was harmful to humans. However, the EPA banned it anyway a few months later. Malaria is now an enormous problem in Africa again, and thousands of people die there because of it. Recent clean air bills concerning cement kilns and coal-fired plants were only passed because 58% of Republicans voted in favor of those bills. The first clean air and clean water acts came out of Montana and were written and proposed by Republicans.

I wonder why no one notices that George Soros who promotes politicians and activist groups that push the climate change agenda, made a large portion of his billions from the oil business and just recently invested $2 million into the largest coal company in the world.

6. Republicans discriminate against women
    "Finally, women will get equal pay." This was a statement made by Hillary Clinton in one of her stump speeches in her attempt to become president in 2016. One of the stories the manipulators use to convince women that they are being discriminated against is, that women don't earn as much as men do. Fifty years ago, this was probably a true statement whether someone was a Democrat or a Republican. Today there are strict anti-discrimination laws that, for the most part, keep this from happening. The statistics show that women only earn .77 for every dollar that men earn. How is this possible? More women tend to stay at home with the children than men do, at least until the children are older and because of the limited amount of working years of some of these women, they are less likely to work their way to the top of corporations. More men work in hazardous occupations such as oil rigs, firefighting, and law enforcement. More men are airline pilots. More men are engineers, probably because men are just more attracted to that type of vocation. More men are surgeons. However, this statistic is changing every day. Male athletes make more than female athletes most of the time because of market demand. An article by Susan M. Heathfield, a Human resources expert, wrote in About Money, that women only earn 77% of what men earn. This is only part of the story. The increase in women working has been substantial in the recent past. In 1950, 34% of women age 25-34 were in the workforce. By 1998, that number

had increased to 76%. Other age group numbers were similar. Susan also reported that women age 20-24 were absent from work 5.6% of the time compared to men at 2.7%. Other factors that affect these numbers according to Susan were chosen studies that are affecting their pay and employability potential. She reports that 1 out of 10 engineers are women. She also reports that 55% of women-owned businesses are in the service industry. Although Susan, I believe is trying to say that it isn't a fair world for women, her own statistics show otherwise. Since 1979, women inflation-adjusted earnings have increased by 14%, but men have decreased by 7% during that same time. Having said all that, look how many Senators, Congress members, governors, mayors, police chiefs, military fighter pilots, and large corporation CEOs are women. Here is a list of some of the top female CEOs in America. Yahoo: Marissa Mayer, Kraft: Irene Rosenfeld, Pepsico: Indra Nooyi, Wellpoint Healthcare: Angela Braly, Xerox: Ursula M Burns, Sunoco: Lynn L. Elsenhans, plus Archer Daniels Midland: Patricia Woertz. Twenty-five years ago, women owned approximately 10% of American businesses. Today that number is approximately 30% and growing every day. From 1997 to 2007, women-owned companies grew at twice the rate of men-owned companies. However, male-owned businesses tend to create more revenue on average because women tend to start more service related businesses.

 Abortion became a women's rights issue and because most conservatives believe that when a baby is conceived that baby has the right to live, means that conservatives are against women. It's interesting that most single women vote Democrat and most married women vote Republican. Although rape, incest, and the mother's health only make up approximately 3% of abortions in America, this is used quite often as a "gotcha" question when a liberal reporter wants to show a Republican as not caring. Liberals will spend millions to build tunnels under freeways for frog migration routes. They will protest about farmers taking water away from salmon that are not native to a certain part of the country. They even fight for insects, but don't think babies at 20 weeks old are worth trying to save. Our culture has changed dramatically over the last 60 years. Until the 60s, a large percentage of women stayed home to raise children, but the age of enlightenment (the 60s) changed attitudes about women working, and therefore, attitudes about pregnancy also changed. As women planned business careers, childbirth had to be put aside. Unplanned pregnancies could interfere with climbing the corporate ladder. With the women's liberation movement of the 60s and the war on Christianity, abortion became an accepted method of contraception. Statistically, 86% of Americans claim to have Christian or Jewish beliefs so using abortion as a convenience would go against those beliefs, therefore, the manipulators changed the story. Abortion just ends an unwanted pregnancy. It's not a baby, it's a fetus or just a blob of cells, so no one gets upset about flushing some cells. There have been attempts to pass laws that would require anyone wanting an abortion to first view a sonogram of the child inside them, but the liberals fought and successfully stopped these laws from being implemented. The truth is when someone gets an abortion they are not just no longer pregnant, they are now the mother of a dead baby. Men, however, are told they shouldn't be part of the discussion because it is not their body that is being affected. Newsflash: Men care about the life of the baby that is being terminated. Why is abortion more acceptable than teaching abstinence and control? Teen-agers can't legally buy a beer or get a driver's license until a certain age, but they can get an abortion without their parent's knowledge. Why do the liberals want to give so much sexual freedom to these young people? These young people will be voting in just a few years. It has nothing to do with women's rights. It has everything to do with controlling votes.

The land of milk and honey

America is a country founded by immigrants. Immigrants who wanted a different way of life. A life that was free from tyrannical persecution or demands to believe in one religion or another, and a life that involved some risk in return for liberty. Millions risked their lives because of the dream that America was. In 1965, the Democrats under LBJ developed a strategy to gain more votes through immigration. Statistically, Latinos vote predominantly democrat, so let's add a few million Democrats by opening our borders legally and illegally. First, let's look at legal immigration. Today there are approximately one million legal immigrants who start a new life in America each year, yet we are told that our immigration system is broken. That is a higher number of legal immigrants than ever before and more than any other country allows. Between 2010-2013 the Obama administration authorized over 300,000 immigrants from muslim countries. Of these immigrants ,91% are currently on some type of government assistance. The government feels it is okay to bring in masses of people who will be dependent on government assistance, yet they can't give seniors cost of living increases on their Social Security benefits. Unemployment has been a major issue for several years now, and there is a narrative that America needs the amount of legal immigrants that are coming in because many of those immigrants are young people who are coming here to become involved in the high tech and science-related industries. We are told that we need these people as if we don't have any young people here who could fill those shoes. The problem with this concept is that over 70% of our young people graduating with degrees in IT or science related curriculums can't find a job. I met a young man named Ken who had a Masters degree in Bio-Chemistry. He remarked that there is now a perception that if you are from Asia or India that you're probably smarter and more qualified for positions in that field. If that's true, why are the most of the new innovations in the computer world from American entrepreneurs? Why do so many of the young people from those areas come to America to get their education? By the way, Ken became a successful real estate agent. However he had to pay back enormous student loans for a degree that he never used.

Since 1965, our borders have become a highway for illegal immigration. The general consensus that is fed to us, is that there are somewhere over eleven million illegal immigrants in America. The number is probably much higher than that. How do so many cross the border? First, the border that runs from Texas to California is mostly rural, mostly desert, and very sparsely populated. Our southern border stretches for 1,954 miles. The job of patrolling that much real estate is very difficult. The number of Border Patrol agents might be enough to maintain some control, however, deployment has been mishandled by the past administration. For example, of the 20,000 BP agents, approximately 2,500 are stationed in the San Diego area of California. In one day in June of 2014, USA Today reported that there were 97 arrests of illegals in the San Diego area. On the same day the 3,200 agents assigned to the Rio

Grande Valley area of Texas, arrested 1,422 people. Why are these BP agents deployed in this way? Welfare benefits have been like a welcome mat to illegals the last two decades. Illegals are eligible for welfare benefits plus they are given in-state tuition for attending college in many states. Their children go to our public schools, and because they have not assimilated into America and learned English, these children struggle to keep up, therefore, schools are forced to have bilingual teachers and classes. Illegals don't buy health insurance, and therefore, they use hospital emergency rooms and very seldom pay for those charges.

So why is this huge influx of illegals such a problem and has now apparently become one of the biggest issues with Americans? Unemployment, crime, and culture. There is a myth in America that illegals take the jobs that Americans don't want. The housing industry is doing well in Texas especially. If you drive through a subdivision where new homes are being constructed, you will see the bulldozer operator, the plumbers, carpenters, electricians, and painters are predominantly illegals who speak very little, if any English. These aren't jobs digging ditches that supposedly American don't do. These are good-paying jobs. Being a heavy equipment operator used to be a high paying job. Plumbers, carpenters, and electricians were usually independent contractors and again were very good occupations. Since these illegals are willing to work for less money, business owners hire them and consequently see more profit in their bottom line. This has resulted in lower wages overall the last few years in our country. Large companies and therefore the U.S. Chamber of Commerce are very supportive of these people staying right here. If you could reduce your labor cost by 20% wouldn't that help your business? And if you weren't having to supply these illegal employees with things like health insurance, sick pay. or vacations, wouldn't that help your bottom line also? See, benefits like health insurance were given to employees to attract and keep better employees, but if you have illegals standing in line for a job then why provide them with benefits? The other jobs related problem with these illegals is how many of the lower paying jobs such as service-related jobs, they are taking that historically a lot of young Black men and women were in. Barack Obama wrote in his book, Audacity of Hope, that the influx of illegal immigrants will harm "the wages of blue-collar Americans". Unemployment with young Black men under 30 is now approximately 40%. Illegal immigration is the single biggest reason for young Black unemployment. This again is manipulation. Latinos make up a bigger voting block than Blacks and therefore if the Democrats can get illegals the right to vote they will absolutely control the vote from now on. There is another myth that these illegals are having to stay in the shadows to keep from getting deported. Recently, if you wanted to hire some day-labor, you could look in the parking lot of the U.S. Post Office in Maypearl, Texas. The U S Post Office! Now they are at the convenience store down the street. Would you call that staying in the shadows? Approximately 300,000 babies are born each year to illegal immigrant mothers in America. There is currently a belief that the U.S. Constitution says that those babies are automatically U.S. citizens. The original authors of the 14th Amendment to the Constitution wrote this amendment because southern Democrats after the civil war did not want Blacks to be able to vote or have rights equal to Whites. This amendment was designed for the recently freed slaves that had African descent and whose ancestors were brought here. This amendment was not designed to give babies from illegal immigrants, automatic citizenship. Actually, it was just the opposite. Jacob Howard who helped author this amendment specifically states that this does not apply to foreigners or children of foreigners. Currently, approximately 71% of the families of these so-called anchor babies, receive some form of government assistance. Hospitals and doctors bear the costs of these births and then pass on the costs to citizens that have health insurance in order to make up their losses.

Although most illegals come to America because of better opportunities than where they came from, there are also many criminals coming across the border as well. Longtime Governor of Texas, Rick Perry, reported that over a seven-year period there were over 750,000 crimes committed in Texas by illegals, including some 3,000 murders and some 5,000 rapes. A disproportionate amount of alcohol-related fatal car crashes were attributed to illegal aliens and in many cases, were hit and run. Approximately 3-5 % of our population is currently illegal immigrants yet in 2014 they accounted for 36% of the federal sentencing cases including 12% of the murders and 74 % of drug-related cases. The FBI reported in Los Angeles County that over half of all gang members are most likely illegal aliens, and that 95% of all their murder warrants are for illegal aliens. The illegals have segregated themselves into areas of our cities where businesses cater to them in Spanish. They have Spanish television and radio. There is no push for these illegals, and for that matter legal Latinos, to assimilate and learn English which keeps them segregated and limits their opportunities. Keep them speaking Spanish. Don't let them assimilate. Keep them divided. Victor Davis Hanson wrote in his book, Mexifornia, that in the past Mexican immigrants wanted their children to become educated and to learn English so they wouldn't have to pick grapes.

Latino gangs, mostly comprised of illegals, also threaten the hard-working Latino families who are trying to improve themselves. The open borders strategy is not a strategy to help poor people from other countries. It is an orchestrated plan to change voting blocks. Right now, illegals can't vote, however when they are counted in a census their numbers can affect the number of electoral votes in a state.

Other immigration issues have come to the forefront recently as well. Immigration from predominantly Islamic countries have raised great concerns because of our governments admitted inability to properly check the backgrounds of these people. In our country, almost everyone has some way to identify themselves, but people coming from some of the middle eastern countries have no way to prove who they are or where they come from. Radical Islamic terrorism is real, and it is foolish for our country to admit people from these countries that have recent histories of promoting terrorism throughout Europe and have expressed their intent to spread their violence to America. The Democrat party passed the Immigration Act of 1952 because of their concern for certain individuals and the real possibility of becoming a threat to the American way of life. Senator Pat McCarran proposed this law and stated, "I believe that this nation is the last hope of Western Civilization and if this oasis of the world shall be overrun, perverted, contaminated, or destroyed, then the last flickering light of humanity will be extinguished. I take no issues with those who would praise the contributions which have been made to our society by people of many races, of various creeds, and colors...However, we have in the United States today hardcore, indigestible blocs which have not become integrated into the American way of life, but which, on the contrary, are its deadliest enemies. Today, more than ever, untold millions are storming our gates for admission, and these gates are cracking under the strain. The solution of the problems of Europe and Asia will not come through a transplanting of those problems in masse to the United States. I do not intend to become prophetic, but if the enemies of the legislation succeed in riddling it to pieces, or in amending it beyond recognition, they will have contributed more to promote this nations downfall than any other group since we achieved our independence as a nation."

Senator McCarran was looking at a different threat to America, communism. The threat is different, but the issue is somewhat the same. There are millions of immigrants that are storming our gates to get into the United States, but they do not want to assimilate into our way of life. Like Senator Mccarran stated in 1952, they want to pervert, contaminate, and destroy the American society. He talked about hardcore, indigestible blocs that have not become integrated into our way of life and are our greatest enemies. We have seen examples of this recently with Islamic terrorists slaughtering innocent Americans to promote their ideology. This law passed in 1952 which is still law today, prohibited anyone immigrating to the U.S. that belongs to any organization that seeks to overthrow the government of the U.S.A. This does not include all that follow Islam, but it certainly includes those that submit completely to Sharia law which does not follow our Constitution or U.S. law. Senator McCarran referred to America as an Oasis. America is an oasis, but it won't stay that way if immigrants are allowed, whether they come from the middle east or some third world socialist country, to push their ideologies into our society and push our ideas of freedom and liberty out. America, as Senator McCarran stated, is the last hope of western civilization. Anyone wanting to immigrate to the United States should have to prove who they are and should have to show how they will contribute to this country and their intention to abide by the U.S. Constitution. Until the government is able to establish procedures that will ensure that anyone attempting to immigrate have met the above-mentioned criteria, immigration should be suspended.

Senator McCarran talked about moving the problems from Europe to the U.S. almost 70 years ago, and he pointed out that this will not fix the problem. The same can be said today. The problems in Syria and Iraq need to be fixed over there. In 1979, there was another crisis involving radical Islam. Iranian college students took 52 Americans hostage and held them for 444 days. President Jimmy Carter took action and deported 7,000 Iranian college students and immediately stopped all immigration from that part of the world. Coincidently within hours of Ronald Reagan being sworn into office, the hostages were released.

Even though the issues we have today are very similar to what Senator McCarran talked about in 1952, and the Iranian Crisis in the 70s, today apparently the Democrat party has decided that votes are more important than the security of the country. Today foreign-born residents make up over 40 million, and that number is growing. Unless this trend is stopped, America will become one of the countries all these immigrants left.

Scratch my back and I'll scratch yours

"Braveheart" a very popular movie with Mel Gibson depicted the Scottish fight for freedom from England. In one scene, the Earl of Bruce tells his father that William Wallace (Gibson) has started a revolution. His father tells him, "You support the revolution from our lands in the North, and I will condemn it from our lands in the South." This scene is much like the games American politicians, both sides, by the way, play in Washington and many times in the state houses also. Oscar Ameringer, a German-born socialist organizer once stated, "Politics is the gentle art of getting votes from the poor and campaign funds from the rich, by promising to protect each from the other."

A very derogatory term, Banana Republic, is an appropriate label for what America is rapidly becoming. This term refers to typically small countries that are run by corrupt dictators who control every phase of their economy, and they manipulate the industry or businesses in their countries in ways that benefit these dictators financially. America won't stand for that! We have laws against that. After all, Martha Stewart went to jail for insider trading. Right?

At the time of the writing of this book, George Soros had just bought one million shares of Peabody Energy. Peabody Energy is the world's largest private-sector coal company.

Do you believe in coincidence? That's what we are supposed to believe, I guess.

George Soros is listed as the 20th richest person in the world. He is one of the largest investors in the world. He was also one of Barack Obamas and other Democrats largest financial supporters. He does this through a super PAC called, Priorities USA Action. When President Obama took office in January of 2008, the share price of Peabody Energy (Jan 28th, 2008) was $59.30. During his tenure, President Obama's administration via the EPA imposed new regulations requiring coal companies to reduce their carbon emissions by 32%.

This new regulation caused the share price of Peabody and other coal companies to plummet.

Here's the coincidence. George Soros bought one million shares this week of Peabody Energy for just over $1 per share. When Peabody Energy emerged from the resulting bankruptcy, their price was $32 per share. Probably just lucky right?

Upon taking office, Obama also declined to approve offshore deepwater drilling permits for companies wanting to drill in the Gulf of Mexico, off American shores because it would be bad for the environment. Here's another coincidence. In 2010 Obama approved a $2 billion loan to a Brazilean owned oil company called Petroleo Brasileiro SA, commonly known as Petrobas, for deepwater drilling. Guess what was George Soros largest investment in his portfolio at the time? You guessed it, Petrobas. Just a coincidence I'm sure.

Maybe just a coincidence but did anybody notice that after President Obama declined the Keystone Pipeline project to go forward, that Warren Buffett's railway company BNSF, stock price soared? Again, probably just a coincidence that BNSF will have to carry all that nasty Canadian oil instead of a pipeline and just a coincidence that Mister Buffett is a big democratic supporter.

General Electric owns NBC which has been Obama as well as most Democrats biggest cheerleader. Jeffrey Immelt, the head of General Electric, was named Obama's Chairman of his Outside Panel of Economic Advisors. According to the New York Times, when GE reported income of $5.1 billion, they also reported that they paid zero Federal Income taxes. I want to hire his tax guy! But I'm sure this is just another coincidence. Speaking of the New York Times, which has historically supported the liberal agenda including support for illegal immigrants, most people are not aware that Carlos Slim, the richest man in Mexico and maybe the world, recently kept them out of bankruptcy. One coincidence after another. It's amazing isn't it?

On January 20, 2001, President Bill Clinton pardoned International fugitive Marc Rich. Rich was on the FBI's top ten most wanted list. He owed $48 million dollars in taxes and was wanted also for trafficking in oil with Iran, North Korea, and South Africa which were supposed to have embargos against them at the time. Rich was ordered to pay $1 million of the $48 million in owed taxes. Rich's ex-wife donated $450,000 to the Clinton library shortly before the pardon, probably just another coincidence, and Peter Schweizer reported in the New York Post that even though Rich died in 2013, his business partners, lawyers, advisers, and friends have showered millions on the Clintons in the last decade and a half. Barney Frank called this pardon, "shameful."

In 1992, Joe Manchin, who was the governor of West Virginia, convinced his daughter to take a job as a clerk in a factory at a pharmaceutical company called Mylan. In 2007, she was accused of inflating her resume to include an MBA that she said was given to her by the President of West Virginia University, Michael Garrison. Garrison had also been a lobbyist and consultant to Mylan. Over the years, Heather Bresch was promoted frequently, and in 2011, was appointed as the CEO of Mylan. Govenor Joe Manchin appointed his wife, Gayle, to the Board of Education in 2007, and in 2010 she was made the president of the National Association of State Boards of Education. In 2012-2013 Mylan spent 4 million dollars lobbying Congress to make Epi-pens available in schools. USA Today reported on September 21st, 2016, that Gayle Manchin also spearheaded an effort to require schools to supply Epi-pens. Since then, Mylan has raised the price of Epi-pens 461%. Heather Bresch is now compensated 18.9 million dollars per year as the CEO. She also owns approximately 100,000 shares of Mylan.

Insider trading is another sore subject, at least for the ones of us that are not part of the U.S. Congress. Our laws allow our politicians to frequently profit from insider trading information without prosecution. Seven out of the top ten U.S. Congress members have made much of their wealth in the stock market. Is it any wonder why they start campaigning for reelection as soon as they are sworn in? Here is a list of the top ten wealthiest members of Congress and where their wealth came from.

1. Darrel Issa, Republican. Current net worth $357 million. Founder of a huge car alarm company.
2. Michael McCaul, Republican. Current net worth $117 million. Married to the daughter of the owner of Clear channel radio
3. Jay Rockefeller, Democrat. Current net worth $108 million. Money comes from the oil business
4. John Delaney, Democrat. Current net worth $101 million. Founder of Healthcare Financial Partners
5. Mark Warren, Democrat. Current net worth $95 million. Shrewd investments in cell phone industry
6. Jared Polis, Democrat. Current net worth $73 million. Made in the stock market
7. Richard Blumenthal, Democrat. Current net worth $62 million. Made in the stock market
8. Scott Peters, Democrat. Current net worth $45 million. Made in the stock market
9. Dianne Feinstein, Democrat. Current net worth $43 million. Made in the stock market and also from Carlton hotels.
10. Suzan DelBene, Democrat. Current net worth $37 million. Made in the stock market.

There is an old saying about talking out of both sides of your mouth. A quote from a politician in a movie said, "I'm a politician, which means I'm a thief and a liar. When I'm not kissing babies, I'm stealing their lollipops." Politicians and celebrities like to vilify the rich or capitalism in general. Yet these same people are some of the wealthiest people in America. Elizabeth Warren stated in a recent speech that "profiting from student loans is wrong. It's morally wrong. It's obscene." Yet Senator Warren charges $430,000 to teach one college course. Hillary Clinton says we have to do something about the high cost of a college education in America, yet according to the Washington Post, when she was asked to give a speech at The University of Missouri she said sure, for $275,000 for 15 minutes! Actors, actresses, singers, comedians, and sports figures enjoy all that America has to offer. Mansions, private jets. and private bodyguards, yet they support communist leaders like Chavez and Castro where the only people getting ahead are the dictators and their supporters and families. Demonize the rich and then tax them more is always their solution. Elbert Guillory, a Black Republican member of the Louisiana State Senate, put it this way, "The King's solution is always the same. Let us tax the rich...and then the rich get poorer. The poor get poorer. And the only one that gets rich...is the King. This was the society that our forefathers declared independence from in 1776."

Last year, Congress passed a budget that includes taking money from the Old Age Fund part of Social Security to give it to the disability part of Social Security because that trust fund is broke. Why? Other than the fund being broke, what is the motivation for the politicians to do this? The Old Age Fund is for seniors. The politicians know that seniors have a limited shelf life so to speak. I'm one of them so I can say that. They can only get votes from seniors for a while. However, there are more and more younger people now collecting disability from Social Security. Many of these recipients are truly disabled and need help. There are millions of people now working the system because of a group of law firms that have figured out how to file suit on Social Security and the high cost of legal fees to fight sometimes frivolous claims is higher than just paying the claims. The Wall

Street Journal reported that the Federal Government paid out over 1 billion dollars to these legal firms in 2014. The Dallas Morning News reported the huge amount of these frivolous claims is clogging up the system which causes people with legitimate claims to have problems collecting. Most claims are now initially declined and then have to wait for a hearing. The average wait according to the Dallas Morning News is now 512 days. The politicians answer is to put more money into this fund instead of fixing the issues with the system. See, every issue always comes back to the same thing, votes.

While we are on the subject of Social Security, let's talk about why the Old Age Fund is going broke. The Social Security Administration reports that at our current level, the fund will not be able to pay full benefits starting in 2033. FDR started Social Security and promised that the funds would never be used for anything other than the Old Age retirement benefits it was designed for. That promise didn't last long. He borrowed from the fund to build the atom bomb. Truman, Eisenhower, and JFK all borrowed from the fund. LBJ and his democratic controlled Congress voted to add the fund into the general fund, and at that point, the so-called trust fund became the largest creditor of the U.S. Government. Today the trust fund is basically just full of IOUs. FDR also promised that Social Security benefits would never be taxable. Today, if a married couple has more than $44,000 of what is called MAGI, Modified Adjustable Gross Income, then up to 85% of their Social Security benefit is taxable. The government takes all this money out of your paycheck every month your whole life to do with whatever they want with, and then when it's time to give it back to you as promised, they say you have to pay taxes on it. Are you getting mad yet? Now, if they were using this money to defend the country or to build highways, most Americans would be okay with that. Your government is giving 20 million dollars of your Social Security money to Indonesia to help them get more Masters degrees. Your government is spending 25 billion dollars a year to maintain vacant government buildings.

Union contributions to our politicians, garner favors from congressmen when bills come up that may affect these unions. Here is a list of the top union contributions and recipients from the last mid-term election.

1. Nick Rahall-Democrat- $403,500
2. Ed Markey-Democrat- $373,000
3. Frank LoBiondo-Republican- $350,150
4. Timothy Bishop-Democrat- $335,750
5. Gary Peters-Democrat-$322,300
6. Steny Hoyer-Democrat-$313,655
7. James Clyburn-Democrat-$311,500
8. Ann Kirkpatrick-Democrat-$298000
9. Chris Bustos-Democrat-$293,350
10. John Turney-Democrat-$285,500

Union members contributions go to these politicians whether the members agree with their policies or not.

The largest union contributor was the Service Employees International Union which is made up of over 50% healthcare workers. This group was heavily in favor of The Affordable Healthcare Act (Obamacare), raising the minimum wage, and they contributed $28 million to Barack Obamas last presidential campaign. Act Blue, a political action committee that allows anyone to contribute to Democrats through the internet, contributed $194,439,211 in the last campaign. Kind of interesting when the media claims that Republicans tried to buy the last election, don't you think?

Interest rates are at historic lows, we are told to help the economy and to help the middle class. Have you noticed how many large corporations have been buying other corporations the last few years? One airline buys another. The largest beer company buys one of the other largest beer companies. The largest pharmaceutical company buys one of the other large RX companies. Office Depot and Office Max are together, and now Staples is going to buy them both. Do you think they use their own money to do that? Why should they when interest rates are so low? This is happening repeatedly across America. So what you say? Why should you care? It's called competition. Competition keeps prices lower. When one beer company buys another huge beer company, guess what? A lot of competition just went away. Expect to pay more for airline travel, and more for your beer, and office supplies in the future. The other problem for average Americans who are trying to save for their retirement is that low-interest rates don't accumulate much over the years. Low-interest rates are good for big banks, big corporations, and the politicians on both sides that are promoted by those groups, but they're not good for people trying to save for retirement. Remember when you could walk into your bank and actually talk to your banker? Well, if you are younger than 50 you may not remember those days unless you live in rural areas. Again, buy up the small banks, and you get rid of a lot of competition, and use somebody else's money to do it. Low-interest rates have boosted the stock market because of the same reason. Why shouldn't big institutional investors gamble in the market when they can use other people's (the Fed) money. The level of individual investors in the stock market is at a ten year low currently. This artificial inflation of stock prices trickles down to the masses in higher prices. It also means there is no foundation to the stock market and with no foundation how can the market withstand storms? There is a term called a "black swan" event. This is a term for something that's supposed to be very rare. When it pertains to the stock market, it refers to what happened in 2000-2002 when the DOW dropped over 45% and then again in 2007-2008 when the DOW dropped again over 45%. Many investment experts are predicting another "black swan' event in the stock market in the near future. The world is in a global economy now, and when Greece, Italy, Portugal, Ireland, or Spain defaults or if North Korea gets ugly with South Korea, or if Israel decides they don't want Iran having nuclear weapons, i.e. someone starts a war, or if there is another real estate bubble burst, this inflated market may crash and crash big. Some of the largest investors in the world are holding record amounts in cash right now. How does this affect the average person? If, and when this crash happens, unemployment will soar. Inflation will soar. Americans are optimistic and tend to have short memories. Remember how you felt in 2008 when you looked at your 401K statement? What if you are retiring about the time this "black wan" event happens, and your retirement account just got cut in half? What happens if you lose your job because the corporation you work for just lost 80% of its value, and you just bought a new home that you can't pay for now. And by the way, your son or daughter will have to get a student loan now for college. Are you getting mad yet?

The U.S. Government has been involved with regime change many times. Why did the Obama administration help to overthrow the regime in Libya but not in Iran? Both countries were dominated by dictator-type countries where the people have no voice. People in Iran hoping to get out from under the tyrannical government begged President Obama to help them but received no help at all, yet he authorized millions for weapons to help rebels overthrow Gaddafi. Why? In an interview in Real News On March 19th, 2014, Horace Campbell, Professor of African American studies and political science at Syracuse University, stated that Libya had 200 billion dollars in reserve and that Gaddafi was threatening to start a new currency for all of Africa which threatened the EURO and the U.S. dollar. Originally the U.S. Government was hesitant to intervene because they looked at this as a plot by the French but pressure from Samantha Powers, Susan Rice, and Hillary Clinton along with Goldman Sachs were able to "build up psychological warfare and propaganda" to influence the media and the American public to believe that Gaddafi was a terrible leader. Gaddafi was a murderer who was behind the bombing of the Pan Am flight over Scotland in 1986. However, Libya was a stable country. Libya is now in complete chaos. Approximately 50,000 people have been killed, and 40,000 have been kicked out of their homes.

The Republicans don't get a free pass either when it comes to this manipulation and outright corruption. Phyllis Schafly, a conservative advocate and many times national delegate, wrote in her book, A Choice Not An Echo, that the Republican presidential candidates from 1932 to 1964 were really picked by who she referred to as 'The Kingmakers." And you thought your vote had something to do with that. This group of "kingmakers" were made up of people like J.P.Morgan, the Rockefellers, and media magnates. This group would get together and decide who to run even if it meant they would run a candidate that they knew couldn't win. Their philosophy was that it was more important to have someone in the White House who was controllable and that wouldn't change the order of things, even if it meant electing a Democrat. Occasionally, a Republican presidential candidate would stand up to these kingmakers, and consequently he was quickly defamed and ridiculed by his own party and then usually dropped out of the race soon after. There was one exception. His name was Ronald Reagan.

Since President Reagan, having middle-of-the-road, go along, and don't rock the boat candidates are again the norm.

"Politicians are the lowest form of life on earth." General George S. Patton

Isms

Socialism, Marxism, Communism, Fascism, and Capitalism

"If all that Americans want is security, they can go to prison. They'll have enough to eat, a bed, and a roof over their head. But if an American wants to preserve his dignity and his equality as a human being, he must not bow his neck to any dictatorial government." President Dwight D. Eisenhower

Why has America, in a relative short time, become the economic leader and center of attention on our planet? Why is India's and China's economy now thriving?
China became communist in the 1920s and even though they had the largest population on earth their economy struggled until they started a hybrid economy allowing some capitalism. India's economy was, and to a certain extent still is, based on a class system where people not only were not encouraged but not allowed to work their way into a better job or better economic situation. Less than half of the population in India has

electricity. That is changing though. They also now have a hybrid capitalistic society.

Despotic leaders have imposed socialism, communism, fascism, etc., on their countries now for over 100 years by convincing their populace that everyone should be equal (except for the leaders proposing this). There is a very fine line between socialism, communism, and fascism. Ayn Rand, a Russian born author and activist, commented about the difference between socialism and communism. She stated, "There is no difference between communism and socialism except in the means of achieving the same ultimate end: Communism proposes to enslave men by force, Socialism- by vote. It
is merely the difference between murder and suicide."
Vladimir Lenin stated, "The goal of socialism is Communism."

Socialism (Merriam Webster) A way of organizing a society in which major industries are owned and controlled by the government rather than by individual people and companies.

A system of society or group living in which there is no private property

Fascism (Merriam Webster) A way of organizing a society in which a government ruled by a dictator controls the lives of the people and in which people are not allowed to disagree with the government

Communism (Merriam Webster) A way of organizing a society in which the government owns the things that are used to make and transport products, and there is no privately-owned property.

Communism and Socialism and Hitler's rise have all been the result of envy or jealousness. The dictionary defines envy as the desire to have for oneself something possessed by another. Another definition states: a feeling of discontent or covetousness with regard to another's advantages, success, possessions, etc. Capitalism isn't fair. It isn't fair for some people to have so much and some so little. The idea of a utopia, a place where everyone is equal, and no one has any worries about money or where their next meal is coming from or the cost of healthcare, sounds appealing to people who often are not getting the results out of life that they want, i.e. a feeling of discontent.

Gerald K. Smith wrote in a magazine called The Cross and the Flag in 1931, "You cannot legislate the poor into freedom by legislating the wealthy out of freedom. What one person receives without working for, another person must work for without receiving. The government cannot give to anybody anything that the government does not first take from somebody else. When half of the people get the idea that they do not have to work because the other half is going to take care of them, and when the other half gets the idea that it does no good to work because somebody else is going to get what they worked for, that my friend, is about the end of any nation. You cannot multiply wealth by dividing it."

Liberal politicians, media, and Hollywood celebrities condemn the rich. They try to convince the ones who are discontent that they are one of them, that they understand their "plight." Actors, like Sean Penn with an estimated net worth of 120 million dollars liked hanging out with Chavez and Castro. The

Clintons criticize the rich from their four mansions that are all worth in excess of 1 million dollars each. The pro-socialism people talk about how evil capitalism is, from their private jets and French chalets or island homes. Singers, actors, and athletes, frequently make $50 million per year, yet they side with the 99% who protest about a CEO, who is in charge of some large corporation with 100,000 employees because he or she makes $50 million per year. Some of these same celebrities talk about human rights and criticize America for not being "fair." Yet they accept millions from dictators famous for human rights violations. Angola is a mineral-rich African country, but in an article in the New York Times March 19, 2015, written by Nicholas Kristof, he stated that President Jose Eduardo Dos Santos, "pillages his country and leaves children to die." He went on to state that 150,000 children per year die from starvation and malaria in Angola. Mariah Carey and Nikki Minaj didn't seem to mind as they were paid over a $1 million each for performing for Santos. Kristof stated that billions flow to a small elite group in Angola while children starve. Likewise, Beyonce and Usher, when they performed at a new years eve party, said they didn't know that Muammar Gaddafi had sponsored terrorist including the bombing of a Pan Am flight in 1986 that killed 270 people. In 2009, Sting performed for the dictator of Uzbekistan who was famous for literally boiling his enemies alive according to an article on VH1 written by Zack Sigel on 12/23/2015. The elite live by different rules apparently.

Stalin, Lenin, Hitler, Mussolini, Mao, and Castro told their people that the government will take care of you. Trust and obey. You want to be a doctor when you grow up? We don't need any doctors right now. We need truck drivers. Doctors in the former Communist East Germany made the equivalent of approximately $30,000 per year. You want to own your home and property. Sorry, the motherland owns your home and property. And the government confiscated all weapons just in case you might object to losing your liberty and this way of life.

Prior to the 20th century, America was predominantly an agricultural based country and economy. And consequently, Republicans and Democrats both had conservative ideas about the purpose of government. After the Civil War, the Democrats were struggling to be relevant. The only way they were winning elections were if they were closely aligned with the conservative values of the Republicans. However, America went through a severe recession in the late 1800s. The south was still depressed by the Civil War and the Democrats realized by completely changing directions they could become relevant again. William Jennings Bryan, though unsuccessful in three attempts to be elected president, began to change the direction of the democratic party. He campaigned about corporations and banks having too much power and tried to show himself as representing the common man. In the book, They Also Ran, Irving Stone criticized Bryan saying that he only acted as a champion of the common man in order to get his vote. In his campaign, he proposed income and inheritance taxes on the wealthy. Does this sound familiar? Even though he was unsuccessful in his election bids, his message of representing the common man became a democratic mantra and class warfare began to have a foothold in America. Farmers and common men struggling because of the recession and looking for an alternative elected a democratic congress. Woodrow Wilson, a southerner, was revengeful about the Civil War and determined to take control back from the Republicans, imposed regulation after regulation on corporations. Most consider

Wilson to be the father of the progressive movement. The amendment that gave the FederalGovernment the authority to impose an income tax was passed by Woodrow Wilson in 1913.

Capitalism is being demonized today. Socialism has reared its ugly head once again. Saul Alinsky wrote a book called Rules for Radicals in which he lays out a plan to change America into a socialist country. Had you ever heard of Alinsky before Barack Obama and Hillary Clinton came along? Probably not. In his book, Alinsky talks about the eight levels of control necessary to establish a socialist state.

1. Healthcare. Control healthcare and you control the people. Hence the Affordable Healthcare Act

2. Poverty. Increase the poverty level as high as possible. Poor people are easier to control. The number of Americans listed as being below the poverty line has increased substantially in the past 8 years. That word poverty stimulates a lot of emotions. An arbitrary line has been established to show people apparently below the poverty line. Although this stigma leads people to believe that by being below this arbitrary line people must be destitute, and although some are, many that qualify to be below this level would be considered wealthy in most countries. Most people below this line have air conditioning, a color television, a microwave oven, and at least one cell phone.

3. Debt. Increase the debt to an unsustainable level. The U.S. Government owes over 22 trillion dollars with no plan how to resolve it. How will the U.S. ever pay this debt that incidentally is owned by other countries?

4. Gun control. Remove people's ability to defend themselves from the government. Remove their ability to defend themselves from criminals, and they become more dependent on the government. In the past couple of years, there have been several cities that have experienced violent rioting, yet the current administration has done nothing to curtail this. It almost looks like the current administration wants more chaos.

5. Welfare. Take control of every aspect of their lives, (food, housing, and income). The total amount of Americans on welfare and food stamps has risen substantially in the past 8 years.

6. Education. Take control of what people read and listen to. Take control of what children learn in school. Regulate what opposing views can or cannot say or print. Ask high school or college students what they know about the U.S. Constitution or the positive things America has done around the world, and you will get a blank stare. The liberals don't want our children being patriotic or believing in American values anymore.

7. Religion. Remove the belief in God from the government and schools. Stop prayer in school. Stop Christmas celebrations in schools. American values came from the Christian/Judeo beliefs of our founders and have been an area that bound Americans together for the last 200 years.

8. Class warfare. Divide the people into the wealthy and the poor. The middle class in America is getting smaller. Rich are getting richer, and as mentioned previously, there are more and more falling into the poverty category.

Hillary Clinton was a follower of Alinsky. Bill Clinton also had some socialist leanings, but Hillary spent time studying under

Alinsky and wrote her thesis about him. Over the last 100 years, there have been numerous people who have tried to get elected running on a socialist platform, but none of them had much success. Recently however, a Democratic politician, Bernie Sanders, a self-proclaimed socialist, was running for president and had thousands attend his campaign speeches. Bernie was running on a platform that offered "free" everything. Although Bernie personally owned and drove a $170,000 car, he constantly talked about capitalism and the inequality in America.

Davy Crockett had a good comment about this socialist situation. He said, "Remember that a government big enough to give you everything you want is also big enough to take away everything you have." Why would some politicians, especially politicians who have become wealthy because of capitalism, want a socialist form of government? Again, it's about control. These elitists don't want to participate in these socialist practices themselves. They want the children of the masses to stay in public schools while their children are in private schools. These elitists want the masses to have government run healthcare, but they all have private healthcare. Historically that's the way all socialist or communist or fascist societies have worked. The masses are supposed to give up everything and just be equal, and the elitists or despotic leaders wind up enormously wealthy.

Walter E. Williams stated, "Prior to capitalism, the way people amassed great wealth was by looting, plundering, or enslaving their fellow man. Capitalism made it possible to become wealthy by serving your fellow man."

"We who live in free market societies believe that growth, prosperity, and ultimately human fulfillment, are created from the bottom up, not the government down." This is a quote by Ronald Reagan.

Capitalism allows someone to reach for the sky. No other country gives people more opportunity to attain whatever their dreams are than America. Major new advances and inventions have come from America more than any other country. Do you think that Henry Ford invented the assembly line just because he was a nice guy? Ray Kroc didn't start a hamburger chain because he wanted to feed the masses. How about the inventors of electricity, telephones, televisions, computers, and air travel? A great number of these ideas that changed the world came about because of capitalism.

 One of the issues that socialist must deal with and eliminate is individualism. Christianity is now under attack because the individual needs to worship his new god, the Government. Religion and patriotism bond people together in America more than any other factors. Some other state mottos show how Americans felt in the past.

 Arizona: "God enriches."

Florida: "In God we trust."

Ohio: "With God all things are possible."

Just like the state mottos that talk about Liberty, these mottos that show how most Americans feel about God have been pushed aside. God is not politically correct. At least the Judeo/Christian God isn't.

So, let's look at some of the reality of the other isms. Russia has been governed under communist or socialist concepts for a long time now. Socialism is supposed to provide a utopia for the people governed by it. Today Russia is still considered a superpower (at least by Russia and the mainstream media). However, this utopian society falls very short of the benefits that we take for granted in the U.S. Benefits such as clean water and hygiene. Only 26% of the sewage in Russia is filtered and cleaned. The remainder is dumped into the rivers and lakes. In fact, 9 million cubic meters of sewage per day are dumped into the rivers and lakes in Russia. Over 500 large urban cities in Russia have no sewage systems. Doctors, lawyers, and other professionals work as waiters where tourists are prevalent because they can earn $500 per month in tips which is much better than the average $100 per month salary they received for their profession. These same professionals live in small apartments frequently with shared bathrooms down the hall.

Like Russia, China has an enormous wastewater problem. As the largest producer of waste and wastewater in the world, it is certainly a challenge to treat this waste. In the rural areas of China, only 6% of their waste is processed. Waste and wastewater is either dumped in the rivers or sometimes the human waste is collected and used as fertilizer in their fields. Kind of makes you think twice about eating food grown in China doesn't it? The urban areas do much better. Estimates show that approximately 77% of waste gets processed in the bigger cities.

France is rapidly developing socialist tendencies. Their unemployment rate and their inflation rate, is nearly twice what the rates are in the United States. Mexico's government model is mostly a socialist type, and we all know how many millions try to escape from Mexico every year.

Denmark and a few of the small Nordic countries have supposedly very successful socialistic governments and benefits. Again, that's only part of the story. Sales tax is 25% unless you are buying a car then it is over 100%. Gasoline is higher in Denmark than almost any other country. Although Denmark is called the happiest country, the suicide rate is twice the rate of the U.S. They rely on the U.S. for protection for the most part, and therefore spend very little on their military. Still, there are numerous immigrants from these countries to America because of liberty and opportunity.

The UK is somewhat socialist now. The UK hospitals buy our used medical equipment. Wow, that system must be doing really well.

Estimates show that approximately 10% of the North Korean population died of starvation in the 90s. Yet South Korea has a thriving capitalistic economy.

The life expectancy for Russian men is 63, and the life expectancy for American men is 83. Inflation is currently running at 14% in Russia. Ask people in Russia, China, and Cuba how they feel about free speech. Ask most people in Ukraine, which was part of the USSR, if they like their liberty or if they would prefer being back under a despotic government where obedience is a requirement. The USSR was supposedly a group of unified nations, but the reality was all the power was in Russia.

Venezuela was one of the wealthier countries in South America until Hugo Chavez turned it into a strict socialist government.

Venezuela was an oil-rich country until Chavez nationalized much of the oil business. Then he imposed 50-60% windfall profit taxes on the oil companies. Oil production is minimal now in Venezuela. Chavez began confiscating all types of companies, banks, and farms in 2007.One particular bank, Banco Federal, which was associated with a television station that was critical of Chavez, was seized in 2010. Owens Illinois, a major U.S. glass bottle company that employed over 1,000 people was expropriated by Chavez. He confiscated over 7 million acres of farmland. The list of seized companies by Chavez goes on and on, but can you imagine any foreign company that might have had ideas to invest in Venezuela still thinking that way? People are now used to daily blackouts because of rationed electricity. Inflation was reported officially to be 56% in 2013. Most believe it is much higher. Venezuelan citizens frequently wait in hour-long lines now for food or basic needs like toilet paper. Yes, toilet paper in Venezuela is somewhat more valuable than money. Yet with all the evidence that socialism has destroyed Venezuela's economy, ABC reported on March 16, 2014, about high crime, enormous inflation rates, and food shortages but never mentioned socialism as the cause. Historically, the leaders of these utopian societies have treated dissidents rather harshly. Stalin was responsible for somewhere between 20 million and 40 million deaths. The killing fields of Cambodia took millions of lives, also. In 1970, Richard Nixon tried to stop the Communist party called Khmer Rouge from taking over in Cambodia. Leftists in America were against any aid and were convinced if the Communist Khmer Rouge took over Cambodia then there would be peace. Jane Fonda told a University of Michigan audience, "If you understand what Communism was, you would hope, you would pray on your knees that we would someday become Communist." The New York Times said the

Cambodian's lives would be "anything but better" with Americans gone. President Nixon and later President Ford pleaded with Congress to give Cambodia $155 million, so they could defend themselves. The Democratic Congress turned off all aid to Cambodia in 1975, and over the next five years, the Communist Khmer Rouge slaughtered over 2 million people.

Some estimates show that Mao was responsible for more deaths of his own people than anyone. Possibly as many as 70 million. Many of these people didn't agree with Mao and didn't want to give up their property or their farms and therefore were starved to death. The politicians trying to direct America toward a socialist form of government will tell you they won't make the same mistakes as these previous despotic leaders. Frederick Von Hayek, a Nobel Prize-winning economist from Austria stated, "if socialists understood economics they wouldn't be socialists." Mister Hayek was a liberal Democrat before liberal Democrats moved so far to the left. Ronald Reagan said, "There are only two places where socialism works, heaven where they don't need it, and hell where they already have it." Socialism never works. Capitalism isn't perfect, but it works better than any other economic model, if left alone. The problem is that our government won't leave it alone. A good example was in the 70s when OPEC raised the prices on oil, consumers reacted. They bought smaller cars and started carpooling. Jimmy Carter thought he had to do something, so he imposed price controls. What happened? OPEC tightened the flow of oil to the U.S. This resulted in waiting lines at the gas stations. Most Americans remember waiting two hours to fill their tank. Capitalism fixes itself. If a bank goes out of business, two more will take its place. Human beings need incentives and competition. Under socialism, there are no incentives. Why should I work hard?

Why should I take risks to start a business or invent a new product? Human beings need private property. Under capitalism, a farmer rotates the use of his land, so the land won't lose its ability to grow products. Historically under socialism people overused land because there was no incentive to take care of it.

Communism, Socialism, Fascism, or Nazism is not about helping the people. It's about control. Hitler and Mao took away the public's weapons, so they couldn't fight back, and Hitler burned millions of books so people in his new society couldn't read the truth. Free sounds really good. But nothing is free! Except in one place. There is one place in America where clothing, shoes, healthcare, food, a college education, and cable television, are free, and everyone is equal. It's called prison.

Thomas Sowell talked about the Intellectual Elite in his book, The Intellectual Elite and Society. These elites believe that the masses or the average person is not capable of making the right decisions themselves. Many of these Elites are from a group of universities which have historically preached against Capitalism to their students for decades. Harvard, Yale, Columbia, and other Ivy league schools have produced more than their share of these Elites. However the socialist or Marxist teachings are spreading throughout American universities across the country today. We need someone like these elites because of their supreme intelligence to make our decisions and therefore take care of us. So they convince the masses that for their own good and the common good, they should allow these elites to pass laws or regulations that tell them where they should live, what they should drive, what they should or shouldn't eat, that they must have health insurance, how many hours they should or shouldn't work, and how to raise their children. Most of these elites like Peter Lewis (Head of Progressive Insurance) support socialist ideas. They don't really intend on being part of these socialist ideas, they just believe the ignorant masses need to be.

Currently, some in America are talking about the possibility of restricting what Fox News or conservative talk radio stations are or are not allowed to say or in some cases maybe should be shut down altogether. In the previously mentioned communist/socialist societies, their leaders also told them what they should or shouldn't read or listen to in the various forms of media. In North Korea the people are restricted to what hair styles they may have.

Why do people from all over the world migrate to America more than any other country? Why do so many risk their lives to come to America? They come here because they don't have the freedom and liberty and opportunities that our capitalistic system has in the countries they are leaving from. They come here because no one tells them in America they can't worship the way they want. They come here because in America if they are willing to work and take chances they can achieve their dreams. In many cases, they came here to flee from communism, socialism, fascism, and Nazism.

Capitalism only works in a good moral society. It only works in a society where people take personal responsibility. America has tried to help other countries that were historically governed by dictators, to become democracies. This has resulted in chaos in most cases. As Americans we are appalled at stories from these countries where the dictators ruled with an iron fist and tortured and killed dissidents, so we stepped in and helped remove the dictators like we did in Libya. Today Libya is completely out of control. Islamic extremists are now in control, and just like several other countries, hundreds of thousands of their citizens are evacuating the country to avoid the genocide which has resulted from the void of a powerful leader.

Norman Thomas ran for president six times, representing the socialist party in America. Norman acknowledged and stated, "The American people will never knowingly adopt socialism. But under the name of "liberalism" they will adopt every fragment of the socialist program, until one day, America will be a socialist nation without knowing how it happened."

The communist party has endorsed the following Democrat candidates for president since 1988.

1988 Michael Dukakis

1992 Bill Clinton

1996 Bill Clinton

2000 Al Gore

2004 John Kerry

2008 Barack Obama

2012 Barack Obama

With socialism, people line up to wait for bread. With capitalism, the bread is lined up waiting for people. Inequality is the new buzz word. Our founding father wanted a land where there is equal opportunity, but not necessarily equal results. Margaret Thatcher talked about the socialist in the House of Commons. She stated, "Socialists would rather have the poor be poorer as long as the rich become poorer."

Symptoms

The healthcare system in America, ironically, has been a very sick patient for a long time, and the patient is getting sicker all the time. Politicians have proposed and sometimes implemented plans that were supposed to fix the healthcare issues such as the cost and sometimes limitations. Whether it is a real lack of knowledge or just playing to the crowd, all the politicians have come up with have been band-aids for this sick patient. No one is trying to cure the patient, they only want to address the symptoms. What is health insurance? Let's cut open this patient and see what is really going on.

One-fifth of our economy is related to healthcare today. The broken healthcare system in America has become a key issue with politicians trying to gain more control. Remember Alinsky said you need to control healthcare.

Is the quality of healthcare going down in this country? Hallmark sold over 130,000 birthday cards in 2010 congratulating people for turning 100 or more. In the past few years, life Insurance mortality schedules have been changed from a top end of 100 years old to 120. Senior citizens are rapidly becoming the fastest growing segment of our population. Our medical community is doing miraculous things today. A few decades ago, if someone was having a transplant, it was on the 6:00 news. There are over 28,000 transplants performed in this country every year. We have, or I should say, had the greatest healthcare system in the world. The success rate for surviving prostate cancer in the U.S. is 84% but in Canada it is only 43%. MD Anderson Hospital, considered by many to be the best cancer hospital in the world, spends more money on cancer research than all of Canada combined.

The cost of healthcare has risen substantially over the past three decades. Some of the reasons were good and some weren't and need to be fixed.

1. During the past 30 some odd years, over 1000 federal and state mandates have been added to health insurance. Mandates like childhood immunizations must be covered. A 64 years old man's policy is required to cover childhood immunizations. Even though that 64-year-old is not planning on having any more children. Therefore, part of the insurance premiums are allocated to the possibility that he might go crazy and get a 21-year-old wife and then have a child. Childhood immunizations are required to be in there. And in case he doesn't want any children with that young wife, his contraceptives must be covered as well. If the contraceptives don't do their job, then well-child care has to be covered. Drug rehab clinics are required to be covered. Even if someone isn't concerned about having any drug addictions, but again the insurance companies must allocate premiums to pay for these possibilities because

some politicians determined that this cost couldn't possibly be born by policyholders. Different states have different mandates. Between the federal and state mandates the average additional cost of health insurance premiums in most states is between 20%-30%. These should be options offered to the consumer instead of mandates.

2. Think about what would happen to the cost of auto insurance if it covered flat tires and oil changes. That's what has essentially happened to health insurance. What is health insurance for? Until the last 20-30 years, if people had health insurance, it was for hospital bills or costs so large the average person couldn't pay them. Unions and the corporate world, however, changed the perception of what health insurance is for. Every time an employee union negotiates a new contract with an employer, they are always asking for more, right? Many years ago, employers began to offer health insurance as a benefit in lieu of higher and higher wages that they would have to pay payroll taxes on. In fact, the health insurance benefits were a write off against their taxes. Once healthcare became an automatic benefit, then ever increasing and improving what healthcare covered became a negotiating tool. Doctor's co-pays for a normal office visit came from employee benefit plans such as HMOs. The average cost for a normal office visit is around $90 and the average number of visits per person per year is 2.5. $90 X 2.5 = $225, hardly enough to require someone to sell the home or file bankruptcy over. The problem is the way insurance works. Whether its auto insurance, homeowners insurance, or whatever, most people never use their insurance, and therefore the insurance company has the money to pay the claims for the few that do. However, when things like office visits or birth control pills are covered, people are most likely going to use

those benefits, and therefore, the insurance company must allocate premiums for those services. The American public has been conditioned because of employee benefits to believe that everything medical, no matter how small the expense, should be included in their plan. There's no free lunch! How much lower would premiums be if these smaller expenses were left to the consumer?

3. In America, we have patent laws to protect an individual or a company from someone stealing their idea and to give that individual or company the opportunity to realize a profit from their idea or invention. That's certainly a good thing. Especially if a company has invested large amounts of capital and time to develop a new product. However, the patent laws need to be looked at concerning prescription drugs. Prescription drugs have become a major portion of the cost of healthcare. If you watch television, you see a new commercial almost every day, about the best and newest drugs. Many of these drugs save people's lives and sometimes make their life less painful and in some cases, make it possible for some people to function. Our current patent laws do not allow for any competition to a new drug for 20 years. Once the 20-year threshold has been met, then generics become available at a fraction of the cost of the name brand drug. The same drug companies sell the same drugs with the same ingredients and the same dosage in Mexico, Canada, and Europe for sometimes 70% less because they have competition in those countries. People tend to follow their doctor's instructions when they are told to take a particular medicine. But many times the doctor is not even aware that there is a generic equivalent. A couple of years ago, a well-known sleep aid with an average cost of over $5 per pill, reached its 20-year threshold. The generic version immediately

came out at a cost of 9 cents per pill. However, the prescription company changed the formula ever so slightly and added a couple of letters behind the name. Presto, they have another 20 years on the new and improved version, and all they have to do is convince the doctors that the new and improved version is much better than the old pill, and consequentl,y much better than the generic. There is a pill for everything, and all it takes is some creative marketing to the public and doctors with some fear thrown in, and we are convinced we must have this medicine to survive. Its easy to understand why these laws haven't changed when the pharmaceutical industry employed 2,500 lobbyists in 2012.

4. Medical malpractice. John Kerry mentioned in his campaign for the White House in 2004, that medical malpractice suits only make up approximately 2% of the overall cost of healthcare. However, there are numerous indirect costs that make that number much higher. In a Huffington Post article doctors explain that they run tests sometimes that are un-necessary just in case of a lawsuit so they can show they did their due diligence. They also showed me that their labor costs are increased because of additional reporting and documentation. One pediatrician from Paris, Texas, recently stated that he has 7 administrative people in his office instead of two, because of medical malpractice and increased government regulations and reporting.

5. Illegal Immigrants. There is a prevarication (lie) in this country that if you don't have health insurance that you can't get medical treatment. That is a completely false statement. You may not be able to go to the doctor or hospital of your choice, but you can receive treatment. In the Dallas area, for instance,

people with no health insurance go to Parkland Hospital, which is the same hospital President Kennedy was taken to when he was shot. And if someone has an emergency, then they can usually go to any hospital and they must treat them. What happens frequently, is when an illegal immigrant mother walks in to a hospital in labor, any hospital, they must assist her with her delivery. They must keep her in the hospital a minimum of 48 hours according to the afore-mentioned mandates. And then 48 hours after the birth, mother and child leave happy, never to be heard from again by the hospital. Who pays this expense? The people who use that facility that have health insurance wind up with charges on their bill for services they didn't receive and frequent double billing. Charging outrageous prices such as $9.00 for two Tylenol, $5.00 for a medicinal access fee (someone to hand them their two Tylenol), and $75 for a tube of Neosporin (regular price around $6.95) are some of the examples how these facilities re-coup their losses from non-payors.

6. Insurance companies are demonized by politicians and the media. Sometimes rightfully so, and sometimes not. Believe it or not, insurance companies don't really want to raise their premiums. They lose customers whenever they do. However, they do have to make a profit, or they will be out of business. Numerous health insurance companies have closed their doors over the years because they didn't have deep enough pockets to remain in such an ever-changing industry. Several health insurance providers have exited the market since Obamacare was passed because of 2014 rules requiring guaranteed issue on all applicants regardless of health. Guaranteed issue is a political tool used by politicians to pull on the heartstrings of Americans. There are an estimated 11 million uninsurable people in this

country. Is it fair to exclude these people from purchasing health insurance? What is health insurance? It is a way to transfer someone's risk to an insurance company to keep from having to pay an otherwise unaffordable medical bill. Health insurance is a service, not a right. In this country (so far) people can choose to take risks. If a 28-year-old young man feels like he is bulletproof and wants to spend his money on a payment for a new Camaro or a big screen television instead of health insurance, then that is his choice. Sometimes things like Leukemia don't care if someone is 28 years old. Now that young man wishes he had bought a health insurance policy, and the politicians and the media blame the insurance company when they won't sell him a policy. Telling a health insurance company that they have to accept a person with a pre-existing condition (that chose a big screen television instead of health insurance) is equivalent to telling a homeowner's insurance company that they must sell someone a homeowner's policy even after their house is on fire. Most states had risk pools in place prior to Obamacare to cover people with preexisting conditions. Is it expensive? Yes, it is. But expensive is a relative word. The payment on that Camaro may be $600 per month, and the premium to the risk pool for a 28-year-old with Leukemia may be $ 600 per month. Again, that's his choice. The media says that there are 46 million Americans without health insurance. Many of those chose to be uninsured. In states where latino illegal aliens are high, the uninsured rate is the highest. This group of the population, for the most part, will not buy health insurance and are happy to use county facilities and emergency rooms for their healthcare. Young people feel paying for healthcare is a waste of money until they get older. Younger people believe that the only reason to buy health insurance is when you want to have a baby.

Now, insurance companies aren't totally blameless either. In order to keep from raising premiums every time there is a new mandate, insurance companies have developed some rather dubious exclusions and limitations in their policies, almost out of self-defense you might say. Many companies have become very skillful with these loopholes to avoid paying claims. Loopholes like sometimes not covering a self-employed person while they are working. Self-employed people are always working! And self-employed people many times have somewhat hazardous occupations. A common limitation which originally started with Medicare is called Reasonable and Customary charges. The insurance company is only required to pay what they deem "reasonable charges." The insurance companies negotiate some of these limits with medical providers and sometimes they just build an in-house schedule of what they determine is reasonable. Very few policyholders read or understand their policies.

7. Good news. Thirty years ago, MRI's didn't exist. Today MRIs, Cat Scans, nuclear heart tests, and so on and so on, tell doctors things that they had to only speculate about before. Thirty years ago, the odds of surviving a heart attack were slim. Today, people live an average of 8 years after surviving a heart attack. Artificial valves and heart transplants are no longer news. Cancer survival rates are getting better and better.

A billboard recently on a highway in Dallas stated someone could get a heart transplant within 7 days.

This is good news, but it is also expensive news. That person who survived the heart attack or someone with a liver transplant, will need regular maintenance. The amazing new tests require very expensive equipment and then someone highly trained to read the test and report the findings to the doctor.

So why don't the politicians talk about these core problems, and what is really happening with healthcare? It is much easier to blame insurance companies for the problem, and then promise to do something about it if you will just elect them one more time. Some governors are getting more federal funds for their state by adding people to the Medicaid roles who shouldn't be there because their income is adequate to pay their own way. Some of our politicians have an agenda to implement socialized medicine, or what is called single-payer, in the U.S. Here are the facts. Take out accidents and murder, and Americans outlive all other countries. Over 79,000 people turned 100 in the U.S. in 2010. One out of every three people born today will live to be 100. The survival rate for cancer in the U.S. is almost twice the survival rate in the UK which has socialized medicine. Average wait for an MRI in America is less than a week. The average wait for an MRI in Canada is 7 weeks.

Readers Digest headlines: Why is Canada shutting out doctors? An article written by Claudia Cornwell, stated that according to the college of family physicians of Canada, 4 million people had trouble finding a family physician in 2002. The country produces fewer family physicians than it did a decade before. In January 2000, Joshua Fleulling, 18, suffered a serious asthma attack in Scarborough. Because the nearest hospital could not accept any more patients, the ambulance took him to another hospital, but he died on the way. The coroner listed acute shortage of physicians as one of the causes of death. Did I mention Canada has socialized, single-payer healthcare? On January 20, 2016, Laura Hillier an 18-year-old high school senior, died from leukemia. Laura was on a waiting list to get a hospital bed. According to Joseph Salerno with Mises Wire, there apparently were plenty of donors identified for the stem cell transplant she needed, however there wasn't a hospital bed available in her Canadian hospital. Have you ever been turned away from a hospital or emergency room in the U.S.?

Politicians know the truth about healthcare, but they use this deception to keep getting elected.

Obamacare was not about healthcare. It was about control. State and federal governments should get out of health insurance.

Education

"Governments don't want well-informed, well-educated people capable of critical thinking. That is against their interests. They want obedient workers, people who are just smart enough to run the machines and do the paperwork. And just dumb enough to passively accept it." George Carlin

What are American children being taught in public schools?

"The children who know how to think for themselves spoil the harmony of the collective society." John Dewey, the father of public education.

 What are they learning about American history or about the Constitution? Most Americans might be quite surprised, that is, if they were allowed to look behind the curtain. Look at Texas, the second most populated state in the country. Texas is a Republican stronghold that was mostly ignored in the last presidential campaign because it was a given that it would vote Republican. So how can the manipulators change such conservative thinking? How can they turn Texas blue? In Texas, without any parents input or even knowledge, the Texas Education Agency adopted a curriculum called CSCOPE. Under CSCOPE, teachers were required to sign a contract restricting them from revealing what is in the curriculum. This program was paid for by public money, but the public was not allowed to know what was in it. CSOPE has done away with math and science textbooks and instead uses the internet. CSCOPE became news recently when parents in a small town close to Houston learned that their children were taught to call the 911 attackers, freedom fighters, instead of terrorists. In a social studies class, teenage students participated in an exercise where the girls wore Berkas and students read from the Holy Quran and learned about Sharia law. Sophomore geography books in Keller, Texas, state that the U.S.A. is predominantly a Christian Judeo nation. One sentence describes the religious tendencies of the U.S.A. The chapter describing the Middle East devotes two pages along with a quiz to enlighten students about the five principles of Islam. Schools across the country are educating kids about Islam in an effort apparently to be politically correct.

What would happen if a teacher had students read the Bible today? This certainly would not be allowed because it might offend non-Christians. In the chapter about Mexico, the same geography book talks about how Mexican immigrants were coerced and forced to believe like the Christians. Ask yourself why this comment would be in this textbook when almost all Mexican immigrants were Christian before they ever came to the U.S.

Previous generations were taught about the positive accomplishments of previous presidents and how these accomplishments helped America to be the greatest country on earth. Very little American history is taught in the public schools and colleges now, and the little bit that is taught, usually is somewhat slanted toward condemning America for much of its past.

Many public school teachers have complained that this new curriculum doesn't have enough emphasis on grammar or spelling anymore. Advocates of the new education argue that spelling is a waste of time because of things like spell check. Cursive writing is no longer taught. Cursive writing is too, "individual."

Today schools put more emphasis on social justice than education.

Although global warming is a theory, it is taught as fact even though there are as many scientists who say humans have nothing to do with the warming of the Earth over the past two decades. Only the scientists who agree with the global warming advocates are given any credence, however. There have been record cold temperatures across our globe over the past few years. The ice in the Antarctic has become much thicker and occupies much more area than ever recorded. Recently, the Washington Post reported that some scientists believe a mini ice age is coming soon. The truth is, our world and our weather, is constantly changing. In the ninth century, the global temperature warmed so much that Greenland was able to be inhabited for the first time in recorded history. The Earth gets warmer and sometimes cooler. The climate change advocates recently reported that the average temperature on Earth over the last year was 0.7' warmer than any year in recorded history. That is less than one degree warmer. Their numbers were qualified as having a margin of error of approximately 0.5'. Al Gore stated to an audience in Germany in 2008 that the "entire North Polar Ice Cap would be gone in five years." The problem with his warning is that between 2012 and 2013 the same ice cap grew by 29% according to the National Snow and Ice Data Center. Al stated that Climate change is causing severe weather events to happen 100 times more frequently than they did 30 years ago. The IPCC (Inter-governmental Panel on Climate Change) which Mister Gore quotes often, didn't agree with Mister Gores predictions. They stated that "there is limited evidence of changes in extremes associated with other climate variables since the mid-20th century. Barbara Boxer stated, after a tragic tornado in Oklahoma, that this is why something must be done about global warming, insinuating that was why there was such a devastating tornado or why there were so many tornados. In the Huffington Post, on December 31, 2012, it was reported that it could be the lowest year for tornados on record. In 1953, a tornado in Waco, Texas, caused 114 deaths, destroyed 850 homes, 2,000 cars, and destroyed over 600 businesses. In 1840, an F5 tornado killed over 300 in Natchez, Texas. Bringing up a controversial issue during a very emotional occurrence such as the Moore, Oklahoma tornado is a disgraceful way of trying to manipulate people to agree with her agenda. Hurricane Katrina was blamed on global warming. In fact, as bad as it was, Katrina is listed as the third worst hurricane in history. In the past 50 years, only two hurricanes were listed in the top 20 worst hurricanes in history.

Here is a list of predictions from the Global warming/Climate change so-called experts:

1. Biologist Paul Ehrlich predicted in the 1970s that "The population will inevitably and completely outstrip whatever small increases in food supplies we make." "And that the death rate will increase until at least 100-200 million people per year will be starving to death in the next ten years."
2. In January 1970, Life magazine predicted, that in a decade, urban dwellers will have to wear gas masks to survive air pollution and that by 1985 air pollution will have reduced the amount of sunlight reaching the earth by 50%.
3. In January 2006, Al Gore predicted that we had ten years left before the planet turned into a "total frying pan."
4. In 2008, a segment aired on ABC news predicted that New York City would be under water by June of 2015.
5. In 1970, ecologist Kenneth Watt predicted that if present trends continue the world would be about four degrees colder in 1990.
6. In 2008, Al Gore predicted that there is a 75% chance that the entire north polar ice cap would be completely melted within 5-7 years.

A study in the journal, Nature Climate Change, reviewed 117 climate predictions and found that over 97% never happened.

There are as many arguments on one side as there are on the other, but because this theory is treated as fact, 300 plus coal plants have been closed and thousands of employees put out of work. Autos cost thousands of dollars more to comply with climate change. Politicians in some cities have passed urban sprawl boundaries because more people living in suburbs instead of big cities would result in more CO2 pollution from more autos. The results of this theory, and that is what it is, a theory, has been thousands of jobs lost and millions spent on additional regulations. On one side, it has put companies out of business, but on the other side, it has made fortunes for the advocates promoting the impending doom and gloom. A group of scientists with NIPSI, recently reported that the slight warming is normal cycles and was not caused by humans. And there seems to be no explanation why this slight warming has stopped since 1997. And, if some scientists and a large portion of the conservative population doesn't agree with the global warming theory, they obviously don't care about the Earth. Once more, this is about control. The manipulators are indoctrinating our teenagers who will be voting in a few years.

 Now, because of the thickening ice and record cold temperatures the narrative has changed. Instead of global warming the catastrophic changes that are purportedly caused by humans is now being referred to as climate change. The culprit is carbon dioxide. Its referred to as a pollutant. Carbon dioxide is what plants must have in order to grow. Plants produce oxygen which they would not be able to do without carbon dioxide. A recent Wall Street Journal article even blamed dairy cattle for some of the CO2 emissions due to the methane gas that was coming from one end or the other. Now students at Penn State are working to develop a supplement that will reduce the flatulence from cattle. John Coleman, the founder of the Weather Channel, insists that the theory of man-made climate change was no longer scientifically credible. Instead, what little evidence there is for rising global temperatures points to a natural phenomenon within a developing eco-system. He went on to say, "I have studied this topic for years. It has become a political and environmental agenda item, but the science is not valid." A climate expert, William Happer, from Princeton University agreed with Coleman. He stated, "The incredible list of supposed horrors that increasing carbon dioxide will bring the world is pure belief disguised as science." So why is this agenda being pushed so passionately by the left? You mean other than money? Al Gore has become enormously wealthy pushing, lecturing, and writing about the impending doom caused by this man-made catastrophe. Our government loaned 500 million dollars to a solar energy group in 2009 which filed for bankruptcy shortly after. Where did the $500 million go? This is about money. The renewable energy industry received subsidies of over $14 billion in 2010.

I believe you will understand the other reasons for this agenda in the chapter titled, the Divided States of America. Recently, new facts that contradict these myths have emerged, yet the believers are convinced that these contradictory facts are not true and just an attempt by the right to cover up the truth. This movement has now developed into hysteria, and when emotions get this high, then facts become irrelevant. The non-believers are referred to as the "flat earthers" i.e. that these people are so ignorant that they probably believe the Earth is flat. Show some videos of a polar bear swimming with a narrative that the bear is having a hard time finding an ice flow and may drown and everyone that loves animals gets emotional and easy to convince that there must be a problem. The fact that, estimates show that polar bears can swim for miles and miles and that there are more polar bears alive today than there were 50 years ago, doesn't matter. The fact that, the glaciers almost completely melted away in the 1800s, long before humans started destroying the planet with their automobiles and such. But as mentioned before, facts are irrelevant. Logic doesn't matter once emotions take control. It's like a scene from John Wayne's movie, "The Alamo" where Davy Crockett (played by the Duke) read a letter to his volunteers that he had written himself but read it as if it had been written by Santa Anna, the President of Mexico at the time. The letter threatened the volunteers if they didn't pack up and leave the Alamo. Davy read the letter to the volunteers to try and make them mad and to motivate them to help with the fight against Santa Anna being waged by the few men in the Alamo. The volunteers reacted just as Davy had planned. However, Davy couldn't let his men make a decision based on a lie, so he told them that he had written the letter, but that he thought that is what Santa Anna would have written. The volunteers were already angry, and even though Davy explained to them that he had written the letter, they insisted that Santa Anna wasn't going to threaten them or talk to them that way.

Worldwide, children are also taught indirectly about the evil from big corporations like the ones from the oil industry, by animated movies that seem harmless and funny. In an electronic world where televisions have so much influence, it is easy to convince the public and teachers that this threat is real and therefore the teachers turn around and show some walruses on a sandy beach to convince their students that humans are bad and must be controlled or the Earth is doomed.

What are children learning about American history? Ask an average teenager about why America was attacked by the Japanese in World War II, and most don't even know that it was the Japanese that attacked America. Ask an average teenager about the Revolutionary War or why the Civil War was fought, and most can't tell you. Ask the average teenager about the Constitution or the Declaration of Independence and most have very little if any knowledge of what is in the Constitution or why it and the Declaration were even written. Ask the average teenager who the current Vice President of the United States is and most do not know. They can't multiply or divide without a calculator, and spelling tests are something they heard about from their parents. Social studies used to be one subject but now seems to be a priority in public schools. Liberal social agendas are now prevalent subjects, and consequently, there is little time left for the fundamentals that were taught in the past.

 The Boston Tea Party participants are now referred to as terrorists in some schools. Patriotism is a thing of the past. Students in Arkansas recently were instructed to rewrite the Bill of Rights because it was an antiquated document. Other Arkansas students participated in an exercise to design a new American flag. America is shown in many cases to be an overbearing country that doesn't treat other countries fairly. Some of this comes from a curriculum called Common Core. State governors were told their federal funds were dependent on their states implementing the Common Core curriculum. Forty-five state Governors complied. Now however, Dr. David Pook, the co-author of Common Core has admitted he built this program because he didn't like the so-called white privilege in our country. The program that was intended to help the minority communities has resulted in lower overall performance in those areas. Politicians use statistics showing America to be behind other countries in math and science, and therefore, if I'm elected, I will do something about education. Almost every major breakthrough in the past 100 years has come from the U.S.A. Electricity, aviation, television, computers, the internet, and many more. Also, the great majority of the medical breakthroughs have also come from the U.S.A., such as artificial hearts and transplants and new medicines. When an Arabic family had twins born conjoined at the head, they came to the U.S.A. for the surgery. India is now a favorite place for people to go for things like hip replacement surgery yet most of those surgeons were educated in the U.S.A.

Students today are only taught about black slaves owned by white people in America. Ask almost any student about black slave owners or about the Irish slaves in America or who, by the way, sold the black slaves to the slave traders in the first place. The slave traders were black and in most cases, were Muslims. Again, half-truths to influence and manipulate.

Some schools include sex education at 13 years-of-age which includes information about sexual preferences such as oral and anal sex. The idea is that they are going to have sex anyway, so they should be educated about it to hopefully prevent diseases and pregnancy. Abstinence is not part of the curriculum. Over 60% of 16-year-olds have already had sex. The numbers of AIDs cases in teenagers has tripled since 2000.

Adolph Hitler said, "Let me control the textbooks and I will control the state."

Children are easily molded, especially if parents are not involved. In some states, a child can get an IUD device for birth control without their parent's knowledge. American youths are fed a dose of Pablum. If you don't know what that is read the first chapter again. This Pablum which is disguised in movies, music videos, video games, but also in the curriculum in our universities, leads our youth to believe that there are no absolutes. There is no black and white. There is no right and wrong. If it feels good, do it. If you are feeling a little insecure and you see a celebrity that changed their sex, maybe that's what you should do, too. Socialism is taught as a beneficial system in many of the universities today. Many college professors across America now identify as believing in socialism or Marxism. A great number of these professors became educators right after graduating from college and therefore have never experienced much of the issues that they teach about, such as building a business. College students are predominantly told one side, and that is predominantly the left side.

America has been built by entrepreneurs. These people decided that they wanted to have more than just a job and they were willing to take chances and work sometimes seven days a week and 16 hours a day to build their business or further their idea. Where would America, or the world for that matter, be if Steve Jobs or Bill Gates hadn't taken the initiative to develop their ideas? What if Henry Ford didn't feel very ambitious and therefore never developed the assembly line to mass produce cars? Or people who developed ways to keep milk fresh for a longer period, so they could sell more? Some would call that greed and say that capitalism is just about greed and competition. Competition is bad. Some schools are now playing basketball games but not keeping score, so no one will get their feelings hurt. People fly across the world today. Do you really think the airline industry would be where it is today if it weren't for competition? Many of our leaders were first leaders on their football team or the valedictorian of their school. Competition teaches leadership. Someone who finds that they don't excel at athletics then frequently turns to something else that they can excel at like music or art. The Federal Government has said boys are now allowed to use the girl's restrooms and locker rooms if they feel more comfortable there. Four states have now passed laws to take any gender identity off all single-stall restrooms. President Obama called on public schools nationwide to allow transgender students to use the restroom they felt most comfortable using. Ask most women if they would prefer to follow another woman just leaving a restroom or some ill-mannered teenage boy who didn't bother raising the seat before using the toilet. Women don't even want to see a urinal on the wall when they go into a bathroom. Also, in California, the words father and mother are being deleted from any public records or proceedings. Instead, they will now be referred to as parent one and parent two. Being a father or a dad is a cherished title just like most women feel about being a mom. When a daughter's first words are "dad," dad won't be able to quit smiling or bragging about that to his family and friends for weeks. Somehow, if those daughters first words would have been parent number one, or two just doesn't stir up the same emotions. Men acting like men, opening a door for a woman, standing up for or protecting someone who is weaker, is looked down on. Most women like their husband or boyfriend opening their door. Most like knowing that their man is their protector. Men and women take care of each other in different ways. I am the proud father of three daughters who looked to me for protection when they were young. Actually, they still do somewhat. When it thundered, they climbed into my lap. When they got their feelings hurt at school, they ran to their mother. Children saying yes sir and yes ma'am, will probably be done away with also. We need to get rid of all gender identity they say. Who is they? It is actually a very small portion of the population who believes these ideas, however, with the help of their trial lawyers and the media, judges and the public are convinced that this is the way it is and should be. This is lunacy that most American disagree with. Educators have a powerful influence on children and youths, and they have a captive audience comprised mainly of young people wanting to find their way in the world and wanting to express their independence. Their professor tells them that socialism is much more fair than capitalism and their young heart just soaks it all in. In America's past, religion was a buffer that kept these young people tied closer to their parent's ideology, but religion is losing its influence rapidly.

Education comes from more than just public schools or college. The environment where someone lives, family, peers, and society all help mold who we are. Older Americans were also indoctrinated. The first songs they may have learned were, "Jesus Loves Me" and "Jesus Loves the Little Children, all the little children of the world, red and yellow black and white, they are precious in his sight, Jesus loves the little children of the world." They were taught there is right and wrong and to go by the Ten Commandments. They were taught to always try your best. They were taught that it's all right to fail, but then get back up and keep fighting. They were taught to respect their parents and elders. They were taught manners. They were taught that believing in God and country was a good thing. They were taught that when someone becomes an adult, they should move out of their parent's house and start their own family and they had to have a job to do that. They were taught to work hard if they wanted to improve their situation. Men were taught to protect women and children and others that can't protect themselves. They were taught to look both ways before they cross the street, never play with matches, and never talk to strangers. They were taught that there's no free lunch. They were taught the golden rule. They learned their morals from their parents and grandparents but also at church and at school. They stood every morning and recited the Pledge of Allegiance. Americans believed that America was a great country. Watching Olympic athletes with their hand over their heart as the American flag was raised or watching wounded veterans in a fourth of July parade have brought a lump into a lot of American throats. They might disagree on things, but all Americans were united when it came to their patriotism. Most television shows had a happily married couple. Movies usually had a good message with a hero. Movies and television today focus on peoples flaws and weaknesses and liberal agendas. Current political issues are written into the scripts of ongoing series to subtly interject the views of the station. Family does not have the importance that it had in the past. Swapping wives was a popular reality show recently. And no one is shocked by a show called "dating naked." Ideas like being a gentleman, or acting like a lady, are not only considered outdated, to many young women that word "lady" is offensive. Young people are very self-centered today. Me, me, me. Oh, wait I need to take another selfie.

Bi-lingual education is now taught in most states. President Dwight Eisenhower worried that too many latinos were moving into America, so he tightened the borders and slowed down immigration which gave the immigrants who had come here a chance to assimilate into the American society. They and their children quickly learned to speak English because that's all there was. Many were able to become successful business owners, consequently. Today, there is a trend to have our schools teach bi-lingual classes because it's thought that latino students will have a more difficult time in English speaking classes. Billboards, menus, traffic signs, product labels, have both English and Spanish. I needed some iodine one day, and when I attempted to read the back of two different bottles, so I could try and determine the difference, I was somewhat shocked when the apparent ingredients on the back of the bottle, in Wal mart in Gainesville, Texas, was entirely written in Spanish. In predominantly latino neighborhoods many billboards and storefronts will also only have Spanish. Is this bi-lingual trend done to help the latinos who have come to America? I don't think so. I believe it is done to keep the latino population somewhat segregated. It is also difficult for someone who doesn't speak English to progress and achieve success, and therefore a larger percentage of these people are more likely to remain dependent on government assistance. Control, control, and more control. Fast food restaurants employ many of these people at minimum wage. Many know little of the English language, and because so much of their world is in their native language, they are not encouraged to learn English and therefore will probably keep serving fast food instead of moving up and improving their situation. If an American moved to Mexico could they demand that their children have a bi-lingual class? Could they get much support if they protested because all the signs and official publications were in Spanish? Again, this is an orchestrated strategy to keep these people from assimilating. Who do you think these people will vote for?

 Possibly the politicians who promise more free benefits? Possibly the politician that promises to get legal status and maybe even citizenship? The latinos who immigrated to America in the 60s and 70s insisted that their children immediately learn English. Some latino children were not allowed to speak Spanish even at home because their parents believed the sooner they were able to converse in English, the better their chances were to become successful. Today, 57% of immigrant families with children receive some form of welfare. Over 90% of Islamic immigrants receive some form of government assistance. Just like the black segregated or latino segregated areas, there are Muslim areas springing up across America that are completely segregated from the rest of America. They are referred to as "Enclaves." Gwynn Oak, a suburb of Baltimore, Maryland is one of these areas. John Yahya Cason, Director of the Islamic Education and Community Development Initiative, explained that western societal tenets clash with Islamic norms. Approximately 400 residents go by strict Islamic moral rules, and the entire community speaks Arabic only. These areas not only speak Arabic, but some areas comply with Sharia law rather than American law. Many of these people fled countries that had no opportunity. Yet their leaders want to turn parts of America into areas just like they left. These people flee from third world countries where government control keeps them from escaping poverty, so they see and hear about all the opportunities in America, so they flock here sometimes legally, and sometimes illegally, with an attitude of doing something special and being part of the American dream. Then someone hands them a welfare check and some food stamps and a television personality speaking in their own language starts telling them that America isn't fair, that the American dream is just for white people. A very smart man once told me, "It doesn't matter whether you think you can, or you think you can't, you're right." The media along with the attorney general lead people to believe that there is a big problem with hate crime being inflicted on the Muslims in

America. The truth is that there are four times as many hate crimes on Jews as there are Muslims, but those stories don't help their agenda, which is to divide Americans and therefore control their votes.

Teddy Roosevelt once commented about immigrants, "In the first place, we should insist that if the immigrant who comes here in good faith becomes an American and assimilates himself to us, he shall be treated on an exact equality with everyone else, for it is an outrage to discriminate against any such man, because of creed, or birthplace, or origin. But this is predicated upon the person's becoming in every facet an American and nothing but an American. There can be no divided allegiance here. Any man who says he is an American, but something else also, isn't an American at all. We have room but for one flag, the American flag. We have room but for one language here, and that is the English language...and we have room but for one sole loyalty, and that loyalty is to the American people."

There is a reason why our coins say, E Pluribus Unum, out of many, one. America is a country of immigrants, but immigrants who, left their country to become Americans. Today there is an orchestrated effort to keep immigrants from assimilating in to America. To be redundant, keep them on the plantation, discourage them from learning English so they won't get a better job, and keep them segregated and dependent, and you will control their vote.

The Federal Government takes substantial amounts of money from every state through taxes for education but only gives a portion of it back to the states and always threatens to with hold the money if the states don't comply with federal mandates on education.

Schools are turning out a generation with little ambition. Previous generations couldn't wait to get out on their own. They were anxious to get a job and get that first apartment, sometimes with a mattress on the floor. It meant freedom and the chance to spread their wings. Today there's no urgency. "I can't find the perfect job, so I'll just stay home with mom and dad," is how many young people feel and many are still there sometimes until their mid-30s. Politicians, the main network television stations, Hollywood, and the schools are teaching young people a sense of entitlement. Colleges are teaching that capitalism is bad. Greed is bad. A car commercial on television talks about not leaving work on time is bad. It says take back your life. Movies and television shows portray parents as selfish and not caring about their children if they work too many hours and are not spending enough "quality time" at home. When I was a young parent, I worked overtime every time I could get it. I painted cars on the weekends. I had my own firewood business in the fall. I did this, so I could buy a decent home for my family. I tried to be the best employee at work and consequently got promoted again and again, and then I paid for my daughter's college myself. And by the way, I never missed a ballgame or a recital or parent's night at school. I was there to teach all three of my daughters how to ride a bike and how to catch a fish. It's called balance. America became the most financially powerful nation on Earth because of our industriousness and our willingness to work extra hard to achieve our goals.

See, the people who spout off about working too hard or who believe in a socialist utopian society, tend to have an envy problem. Somewhere a guy is in his car at 5:00 driving home and listening to the radio and he hears Johnny Paycheck's big country-western hit, "Take this Job and Shove It." And he shakes his fist and yells out "that's right!" Then that weekend he's at the lake sitting on the bank fishing watching the nice boats go by, and on the way home he gets passed by a new car he wished that he had. Then on television he sees a show or hears a commentator criticizing work-a-holics and greedy people. He says things like, I could have all those things if I wanted, but I'm not willing to sacrifice my family time. Liberal Democrats make corporations and CEOs into villains. The same liberal Democrats that are worth millions themselves. Working and achieving and having ambition are now dirty words. Now, the intellectual elite look at this altogether different. The socialist utopian everybody is equal philosophy is for the masses. The elites still want their mansions and millions. Vice President Joe Biden was seen wearing a golf shirt from a golf club that costs approximately $500,000 to join. VP Biden was wearing this shirt at a minimum wage rally. The Clintons claim to be "broke" when leaving the White House but now have estimated worth of approximately $100 million and they own four mansions, with the least expensive one being worth over $1 million. Al Gore had a net worth of approximately 10 million dollars when he left office, but now after several years of promoting his global warming agenda his net worth has jumped to approximately $100 million.

The high cost of college education is currently an issue being discussed as part of the political campaigns. Why has the cost of college increased so much the past couple of decades? The cost of a college education has increased 1,120% since 1978 according to Andrew Rossi of the Daily Beast. The cumulative student debt in the U.S. is over one trillion dollars with the average per student at over $39,000. The cost of a typical college education has gone up 70-77% just in the past five years.

Why are colleges charging so much more than they used to? Because they can. Availability of student loans has increased substantially over the past three decades and especially over the past decade. State aid to colleges has decreased 29% from 2002 to 2012, however, tuition has increased 44% during that same time frame. In addition to these statistics, Bob Hildreth, the founder of Fuel Education, also states that the plentiful student loans available encourage states to cut aid and colleges to raise tuition. A recent study from the National Bureau of Economic research, written by Stephanie Riegg Cellini and Claudia Goldin, compared for-profit universities in five states where some schools were eligible for federal student loans and grants, and some were not. The study showed that the average cost of the universities that had access to federal student loans were 78% higher than the schools that did not have that access. They are charging more just because they can. When states cut their funding, students turn to more federal loans and grants which drives the cost higher and higher. I recently heard a young couple call into a radio talk show to talk about their debt. This 30-something couple was earning combined $70,000 per year and were paying off a $45,000 student loan. Another problem that the Federal Government caused and is now expected to fix!

The media and politicians today act as if it is a tragedy if a young person doesn't go to college. Welders, truck drivers, and entrepreneurs, make more money than most college students during their career. Why aren't those skills promoted anymore?

Now, our education system is focused sometimes on agendas instead of focusing on teaching our children skills and knowledge that will help them achieve their goals when they

are grown. Statistics show pitiful results in fundamentals. The Detroit, Michigan, public school system is $515 million in debt, (Democrat administration), and ranks among America's worst-performing students. Oakland, California, (Democrat administration) shows that only half of their third-grade students can read at grade level, and only 34% of middle school students are proficient at math. Computers, the internet, and calculators have taken the place of learning how to add, subtract, multiply, and divide.

Would it bother you to know that a recent study showed that over 30% of teachers of public schools in the largest urban cities in America send their own children to private schools?

Nationwide public school teachers are almost twice as likely as other parents to choose private schools for their own children, according to the Thomas B. Fordham Institute.

In Philadelphia, 44 % of the teachers put their children in private schools. The Washington Times reported in 2004, similar trends across the country.

The percentages are even more disproportionate for politicians.

Our new God

The Federal Government has become the new God for many. The dividers help people to find a new religion to believe in. Climate change, gay rights, animal rights, or the war on women becomes a religion to many. They need someone to lead the charge, however, and that's where the elite come in. The politicians and the elite believe that they are smarter and superior to most and therefore more capable of deciding what is good for the masses. And the masses willingly follow along. Therefore, it is incumbent on them to rule. Judeo-Christian beliefs have become outdated. Working hard and becoming successful has become outdated. Dependence on Uncle Sam is the new normal. The government causes many problems then the citizens expect the government to fix the problems it created. So the government starts a new agency to fix the problem that some other agencies caused. Case in point is healthcare. Obamacare was an attempt to fix what the government broke. The main causes for the high cost of healthcare was the Federal and state government. As I mentioned in the chapter called Symptoms, the Federal and state government imposed over 1,000 mandates on insurance companies that add approximately 30% to an average premium. Then, in order to keep premiums down, the insurance companies look for cost reduction strategies like higher deductibles and loopholes. Loopholes like policies only paying "reasonable and customary" charges came about because of Medicare. The costs of autos have skyrocketed because of safety and environmental rules imposed on car companies. There are airbags all over the cars now. The government supplied weapons to the Afghans to use against the Russians, and then the Afghans used those same weapons against the U.S. The government made trade with Mexico easier through NAFTA ,and then complains that all the big corporations are moving all their factories there. The politicians no longer work for the people, they govern the people. They rule the people. Recent polls show that over 80% of Americans believe the government has become too powerful and too controlling. Some of the Democrat politicians believe the Constitution is an antiquated document which restricts them from doing what they must. Their egos are so out of control. They believe they are smarter than a document and a system that has formed America to lead the world. America's economy is the driving engine of the world's economy. America's power in the past 60 years has kept over-aggressive countries or power-hungry leaders in check. America has been a model for the rest of the world to follow, until recently.

Alexis De Tocqueville wrote about democracy, "Democracy extends the sphere of individual freedom, socialism restrains it. Democracy attaches all possible value to each man, socialism makes each man a mere agent, a mere number. Democracy and socialism have nothing in common but one word; equality. But notice the difference; while democracy seeks equality in liberty, socialism seeks equality in restraint and servitude." John Kennedy said, "The rights of man come not from the generosity of the state, but from the hand of God." Whether you believe our rights are God-given or not, they are our rights. We are not given these rights by the government. Conditioning is rapidly changing attitudes in this country. When something bad happens, people cry out, "Why didn't the government do something about this?" Individual responsibility is rapidly becoming non-existent. In past decades we look with astonishment at the horrible ways that people in communist countries were controlled, yet we are giving up our liberty to our politicians every day, little by little. This was supposed to be a country that was run by "the people." I believe the people lost control a long time ago.

Cass Sunstein, who President Obama appointed to be the head of the Office of Information and Regulatory Affairs, proposed in 2008 that the U.S. Government should employ teams of covert agents to infiltrate groups who advocate views that Sunstein deems "false conspiracy theories" about the government. In other words, if you don't trust what the government is doing, and you voice your opinion about it then someone may be looking into what you may or may not be doing. The Blaze reported that in an article titled "Open Brain Insert Ideology" Sunstein recently wrote for the Bloomberg View, he cited a study of reforms to the Chinese education system that seemingly proves curriculums can be "explicitly designed to transform student's political views." He asks, "Suppose an authoritarian government decides to embark on a program of curricular reform, with the explicit goal of indoctrinating the nation's high school students. Suppose that it wants to change the curriculum to teach students that their government is good and trustworthy, that their system is democratic and committed to the rule of law, and that free markets are a big problem." He goes on to explain that China started this program in 2001 when they significantly changed textbooks for high school students. Sunstein questions how effective this reform would work in a nonauthoritarian country." Is this conclusion limited to authoritarian nations? In a democratic country with a flourishing civil society, a high degree of pluralism, ample room for disagreement, and dissent-like the U.S.-it may be harder to use the curriculum to change the political views of young people. But, even in such societies, high schools probably have a significant ability to move students toward what they consider a correct worldview, a correct view on life, and a correct value system" Cass Sunstein who was Samantha Power's (Obamas Ambassador to the UN) husband was clearly advocating indoctrinating our high school students to believe that capitalism is bad. The Eagle Forum reported that Sunstein advocates for human euthanasia. In June 2003, he published a paper, "Lives, Life Years, and the Willingness to Pay." He argues that human life varies in value! He states, "I urge that the government should indeed focus on life-years rather than lives. A program that saves young people produces more welfare than one that saves old people." This man was appointed as a Czar by Barack Obama! Dr. Ezekiel Emanuel, the brother of Rahm Emanuel, is a member who will serve on the Federal Coordinating Council for Comparative Effectiveness Research, which has already been approved and signed into law. Dr Emanuel has written similar statements about why healthcare should be rationed for the elderly. These are the people Barack Obama had plugged into his administration. If you stood up and questioned this administration, you might have found yourself becoming a target. "Dinesh D'Souza made two movies about Barack Obama to show why he does the things he does and consequently when he loaned $20,000 to some friends so they would contribute to a certain candidate, he was charged with violation of campaign election laws and sentenced to prison.

Members of Congress, the Senate, plus the Supreme Court and even the President have forgotten that they are supposed to be our employees.

Gun control

"Each of us has a natural right to defend his person, his liberty, and his property." This is a quote by Frederic Bastiat, a French classical liberal theorist and political economist from the early 1800s. The controllers want you to depend on the government instead of yourself. In World War II, the Japanese briefly considered invading America until it was acknowledged that everyone there owns a gun. History shows every country has been invaded at some time, but no one has dared to invade America in over 200 years. We won our independence from Great Britain because everyone owned a gun. Even before we had an organized army, there was a colonial behind every tree with a gun.

As mentioned earlier, the great manipulators use emotions instead of logic or rational thinking, to make their point. Thomas Paine said, "To argue with a person who has renounced the use of reason is like administering medicine to the dead." Murder rates in America are tragic, there is no denying that. Approximately 12,000 to 16,000 murders occur in America each year. Numerous school shootings the past few years have helped the manipulators turn some people's minds that normally wouldn't consider going against our Constitution. After all, who wouldn't be emotional about school shootings?

England is used many times to try and show what happens when the populace is disarmed. The United Nations have become involved with trying to abolish our right to own firearms.

What is the truth? Would it make us all safer if we didn't have the right for an individual to own a firearm? Would the murder rates go down if a law was passed and Americans could no longer go to their favorite sporting goods store and buy a gun? Would stricter gun laws reduce gun violence?

The number of murders in America once again is around 12,000-16,000 per year. However, before most states passed concealed carry laws the murder rate in America was around 23,000 per year. Numerous occurrences happen where people with conceal carry licenses were able to stop murders, but very little attention is given to these stories because they don't fit the great manipulator's story. A UCLA professor, James Q Wilson, an expert on crime, guns, and police practices stated, "We know from census bureau surveys that something beyond a hundred thousand uses of guns for self-defense occurs every year." The Department of Justice estimates that 1.5 million people per year defend themselves at some time with a firearm. This is never reported. A 13 year old boy home alone in South Carolina heard someone breaking into his backdoor. He fired through the door and wounded the intruder who fled. A young mother was interrupted while breast feeding her four-month-old son, by two men breaking into her home. The men shot her twice, but she fired back with her own firearm wounding the intruders and causing them to flee. The two, who had extensive criminal records were arrested later. Then there is Jeanne Assam. On December 9, 2007, Matthew Murray walked into the New Life church and began shooting people. He killed four people and wounded four others before Jeanne, an off-duty police officer, shot him several times, which saved countless lives. You never saw these stories on the mainstream news, did you? There are hundreds of these stories every year, but they don't help the anti-gun groups which are promoted by the mainstream media, and therefore, are very seldom reported. President Reagan once remarked, "The gun has been called the great equalizer, meaning that a small person with a gun is equal to a large person, but it is a great equalizer in another way, too. It ensures that the people are the equal of their government whenever that government forgets that it is a servant and not master of the governed." James Holmes, the theater shooter, intended to do his mayhem at the Denver International Airport, but then thought better because there were armed police there. The people with concealed carry licenses are part of the problem, aren't they? Less than 1% of concealed carry license holders have ever committed a crime. The laws are very strict with these licenses. In fact, licenses can be revoked due to violations such as DUIs.

Did the murder rate go down in England when the government confiscated everyone's firearms? It did not. What has increased in England is the amount of daytime burglaries and robberies. Mexico, Brazil, and 87 other countries, have very strict gun laws but have much higher murder rates than America. In Honduras, a country with a population of approximately 8.2 million, gun ownership is banned completely. Honduras has the highest murder rate in the world. Switzerland, a country with a population of approximately 8.2 million, has a very positive gun culture. There are approximately 45.9 guns per 100 residents in Switzerland. Switzerland has the lowest homicide rate in the world.

The school shootings were horrible. Why haven't any of the mainstream television stations pointed out that almost without exception, these killers were on mind-altering drugs that were prescribed to them to help with some type of mental or behavior issues such as depression? Why hasn't the media said anything about the fact that mass shootings tripled under President Obama? Assault weapons became the focal point after the school shootings. In 2011 there were 323 people killed by a rifle of some kind in the U.S. Although it received no press, 496 people were killed by hammers or clubs of some kind during the same time. When one of these horrific events happened Democrats never failed to take the chance to talk about gun control and that more laws were the answer. They typically only did this whenever the shooter was white. Democrats were noticeably silent when a Muslim attacked and killed four Marines in Tennessee. When police officers were murdered just because they were police officers, Democrats were noticeably silent. When there are sometimes 10-15 people murdered in one weekend in places like Chicago, once again Democrats were noticeably silent. Politicians and celebrities advocate for more gun control while they are surrounded by armed guards everywhere they go. This narrative is not about saving lives, it once more is about control. An out of control government has a hard time controlling their citizens when they are armed.

Chicago and New York have some of the toughest gun laws, but they lead the list of most murders in the U.S. New Jersey has established strict gun laws yet Newark, NJ's murder rate has increased in the recent years. If you subtract the major urban areas that have strict gun laws, America is near the bottom of the list for murder rates. Approximately 35% of murders in America do not involve firearms and between 70-90% of murder victims have prior criminal records. What is our government doing to counter this crime? In Milwaukee, Wisconsin, Dontray Mills purchased 27 guns with a fake ID, and then sold them to felons. He was arrested in April 2014. After being charged with 55 counts of federal gun trafficking, the Obama administration Department of justice negotiated a plea bargain. U.S. District Judge Rudolph Randa stated, he realized the seriousness of the offense and acknowledged the problem of guns winding up in the hands of people who use them to commit violence, but then said that Mills didn't seem like the typical defendant, and because he had ambition to become a rap artist Judge Randa decided that a sentence of one year probation was appropriate. By pleading guilty to one count, Dontray Mills who was charged with selling guns to felons, received probation. Judge Randa stated that "people kill people." "Guns don't kill people." Judge Randa said, "Mills has accepted responsibility."

The ATF recently reported that federal gun prosecutions were down 35% under President Obama took office. Maybe enforcing the existing laws might make more sense than writing some new ones.

The point is that criminals and mentally ill persons or people who are using mind altering drugs, don't go by the rules. Stricter laws would only affect the people who are legally carrying a firearm because they want to protect themselves. 60% of homicides are suicides. 80% of murders are gang-related. If you subtract the gang-related murders and the suicides from the totals, that leaves less than 2,000 murders by guns per year out of a population of over 300 million. The facts are, that there are tremendous gang problems in America's inner cities that many believe the welfare system that crippled the families in those areas is responsible for. They are killing each other over turf, or who is in charge of the drug business, and sometimes just because some politician or reporter stirred them up to the breaking point. A recent young man stated that when he woke up, he knew he needed to kill somebody that day. Why doesn't the government crackdown on these gangs? Why aren't the leaders of this great nation having town hall meetings and using their influence to help families to turn their youth around? Why isn't more being done on the border to do something about the flood of cheap heroin that is one of the main causes of gang-related deaths?

There is also a problem in America that parents don't know what is going on with their kids because they have turned them over to a computer and a television to raise. Any day, you can see SUVs going down the highway with a movie playing in the backseat for the kids. You see families in restaurants, and everyone is on their IPhone instead of speaking to each other. These same parents don't want to actually act like parents when there are some issues, so they also turn their kids over to a doctor who prescribes Zoloft or Wellbutrin or something that calms the kid down, they hope. They don't ask, what are the side effects? How will this change my child's personality? In an article from the Academy of Child and Adolescent Psychiatry, written by Steven P. Cuffe, M.D., the Center for Disease Control reported that anti-depressant use is up 400% since 1988 and that 11% of all Americans over 12 years of age are taking anti-depressants. In 2003 the FDA warned physicians about the possible increased risk of suicide and other harmful behavior among adolescents taking anti-depressants. Suicides are up 30% in that same time frame. The article went on to say that a second hypothesis concerns possible side effects of anti-depressants, such as agitation, impulsivity, and disinhibition. Disinhibition is defined by Wikipedia as " a lack of restraint manifested in disregard for social conventions, impulsivity, and poor risk assessment. Disinhibition affects motor, instinctual, emotional, cognitive, and perceptual aspects with signs and symptoms similar to the diagnostic criteria for mania. Hypersexuality, hyperphagia, and aggressive outbursts are indicative of disinhibited instinctual drives."

It further stated that anti-depressants have been found to sometimes precipitate manic episodes.

Several of the mass shooters over the past few years were taking Suboxone, which is a narcotic with some nasty side effects such as extreme depression, irritability, and mood swings. These side effects become worse if mixed with other drugs. Suboxone use in America exceeds Viagra according to a New York Times article. The article went on to say in 2010 and 2011, a federal study showed there were more young children hospitalized because of "accidental" ingestion of Buprenorphine (Suboxone) than any other medication. In an article from a site called Narconon, they reported that a doctor who treats opiate addicts in Palm Beach, that prescribes Suboxone, noted that small doses will block the great majority of a person's ability to feel emotions while larger doses will make a person practically numb. CBS News reported on June 22, 2015, that Dylann Roof, the suspect in the deadly shooting at the Emanuel AME Church in Charleston, had been previously arrested for felony possession of Suboxone. Stephen Paddock, the Las Vegas shooter was taking Diazepam. Devin Kelley the Southerland Springs church shooter was taking Tramadol, Celexa, and Trazodone. Some of the side effects listed for these drugs are Suicidal thoughts, dizziness, confusion, anxiety, panic attacks, hostility, engaging in dangerous activities and other unusual changes in behavior. These are called mind altering drugs for a reason. The FDA states that these drugs can cause aggressive behavior, manic episodes, and psychotic symptoms like hallucinations. Again, some people have trouble functioning without some medical help, but a lot more kids and adults are on drugs than are necessary and many times like Devin Kelley, they are mixing these drugs which increases the side effects. A pill fixes the symptom. It's helps to control an unruly kid. But then, one day the kid snaps for no reason. Was it the Zoloft, Ritalin, Suboxone, mixture along with a daily dose of extremely violent and graphic video games and some parents who didn't have time to see what their kid was planning? Was it the anger that the media cultivates on top of a dose of psychotropic drugs that many times cause worse depression and aggression? No, it must have been the gun.

When a politician or the media need to cultivate or aggravate emotions, it helps to have an enemy. Hitler used the Jews as an enemy. The enemy for many Americans has now become the wealthy. The enemy for the more gun restriction advocate people has become the NRA. The National Rifle Association has proposed ways to address mental health issues but were ignored by the past administration. The NRA represents lawful gun owners. The bad guys who commit 99% of all the shootings and murders in this country are not NRA members. Murders are caused by people who don't care about laws. Legal Gun owners are portrayed as radical redneck country hicks who can't wait to kill something or someone. In John Lott's book, "More Guns, Less Crime." he points out that as the number of legally bought firearms has increased, the amount of violent crime has substantially decreased. Since 1991, Americans have bought 128 million firearms, and the murder rate has decreased 52% in that time. The anti-gun advocates want you to believe that is just a coincidence. President Obama said that people thinking that he wanted to take away our guns was just a conspiracy. Yet there were a lot of signs that pointed that way. Doctors who accept Medicare now ask if there is a gun in the house. More and more laws are passed to identify who owns guns. That was the first step that England took before confiscating everyone's weapons. Australia had a mass shooting in 1996 where 35 people were killed. Twelve days later their congress passed sweeping gun laws. Semi-automatic weapons were part of a buyback program, and new laws were enacted wherein someone must explain and show why they need a weapon before they can purchase a weapon, and self-defense is not one of the approved reasons.

The statistics show that if you subtract the gang-related homicides and suicides, that the murder ratio per 100,000 people from firearms in the U.S. is a minuscule number.

 Historically, other countries have confiscated guns from their citizens such as the Soviet Union which then exterminated 20 million dissidents. Turkey established gun control in 1915, and then exterminated 1.5 million Armenians. We all know what happened with Hitler when first he unarmed his citizens then murdered somewhere around 6 million Jews. In Uganda, guns were confiscated in 1970, and between 1971 and 1979, 300,000 Christians were rounded up and exterminated. There are numerous other examples of governments taking guns away from their citizens and then forcing ideologies on then with whatever means it took. Americans don't believe such a thing could happen here. And keeping the guns will make certain that it doesn't. Every President, Senator, Congressmen, governor, and celebrity is protected by guns. Shouldn't all Americans have the same right?

Gun laws have been a boon to the emotional influence of politicians over the past few years, and one of the tools they use to divide Americans. Every time some disturbed young man slaughters some innocent people, immediately, some politicians will jump at the chance to gain some points against the constitutional right to keep and bear arms. Why did the founding fathers insist on the second amendment? As mentioned before, they came from countries where despotic leaders or tyrants ruled over them and took their freedom. Not only did the founding fathers believe someone had the right to defend themselves and their families, but they also had the right to stand up against a despotic government that might come along in the future that would try and take away their freedom. There is a narrative that gun violence is getting worse. With the exception of the last two years of the Obama administration, this couldn't be farther from the truth. In every state where concealed handgun laws have been passed, the murder rate has gone down. That is until 2015.

The idea that mass murder is on the rise is also false. During 1957-1958, Charles Starkweather with the help of his 14-year-old girlfriend, killed 11 people. Some were shot. Some were stabbed, and some were strangled. In 1980, Priscilla Joyce Ford killed six people with her car. The worst school massacre in U.S. history happened in Bath. Michigan in 1927 where 44 people, adults and children were killed by an explosive.

Compare Houston, Texas to Chicago, Illinois. These cities are both large metropolitan cities with similar diverse populations. Houston, like most of Texas, allows concealed carry of firearms and has an abundance of gun stores. Chicago, until recently, did not allow CHL and had very few gun stores. Chicago's murder rate in 2012 was 9 times the rate of Houston. The other myth once again is that people who have legal concealed carry licenses can't wait to shoot someone. Thousands of violent crimes have been stopped by these people, but that news is not reported by the network television stations and therefore not known by most Americans. A case of politicians doing one thing but saying another is the case of Senator R. C. Soles. This Democrat Senator from North Carolina who fought against people's rights to own firearms, shot one of two intruders who broke into his own home. One of the other untold stories about the recent mass shooters is that almost every one of those shooters and their parents voted Democrat.

John F. Kennedy stated, "Today we need a nation of minutemen; men who are not only prepared to take up arms, but citizens who regard the preservation of freedom as a basic purpose of their daily life."

The Divided States of America

I chose to start the history of this manipulation 100 years ago because the democratic machine has basically had a 100-year game plan to achieve their goals. Today's Democratic party has a structured game plan that their party seems to always be united in. The main three television networks, mainstream publications as well as numerous activist groups are also strongly united in this game plan. The Republican party doesn't seem to have a structured plan. They only react and try to oppose the Democratic plan. What is this plan? How is it that the Democrats have taken control of numerous groups within the American population? Until the last two decades, most Americans grew up hearing, United We Stand, Divided We Fall. For a long time, it was thought that Americans could disagree, but in the end, they were all still Americans. Even that idea, that America is united behind one flag, is now being challenged by the left.

The Democrats tend to be monolithic and figured out that many Americans, likewise, because of emotions or selfish situations, focus on one issue when it comes to their political stance. They discovered, if you divide the masses by these issues and with the help of leftist leaning media, you convince the masses that your opponent is on the wrong side of that one issue, then you control that vote. Just before World War II, in one of his fireside chats, FDR called these dividers, undiluted poison. Such issues as race, abortion, gay rights, women's rights, religion, morality, union membership laws, global warming, immigration, and gun laws keep people divided. Many of these people believe in lower taxes and less government in their lives, however they become passionate about their one issue. If someone has family who came here from Mexico, then the immigration issue is their main issue even though socially and morally most latinos would match the Republican party more than the Democrats. Most latinos refer to abortion as murder. Most latinos don't want to pay higher taxes. Yet the majority of latinos vote Democrat.

Class warfare divides people by their financial situation and causes lower income people to resent those that have prospered. In the past, this game plan has also focused on seniors. However, there has been a switch in the manipulator's strategy now because they see young people being easier to persuade about moral issues, and also if these young people stand with the Democrats they will be the future of the Democratic party. Anything consequently, that tends to unite the Republicans, becomes a target for the dividers. Since the start of the United States, religion has played a major role in how Americans, especially conservative Americans, made their decisions about social and moral behavior and consequently politics. Pastors, preachers, ministers, priests, and rabbis had an enormous amount of influence on their church members. These entities or organizations are typically set up as nonprofit groups and therefore are not subject to federal income tax from member's donations. Two nonprofit groups in Texas were trying to stop the Lyndon Johnson socialist machine in his 1954 run for re-election in the Senate. Therefore, he proposed and got a law passed that would cause groups to lose their nonprofit status if they used their influence politically, which included churches. Taking prayer out of schools, not allowing crosses to be on government property, stopping military chaplains from talking about Jesus, and the moral decay in our entertainment industry is rapidly eroding the Christian Judeo influence in America. President Reagan stated, "The Constitution was never meant to prevent people from praying. Its declared purpose was to protect their freedom to pray".

Brock Chisolm, the first Director General of the World Health Organization, said in 1946, "To achieve world government, it is necessary to remove from minds of men their individualism, loyalty to family tradition, national patriotism, and religious dogmas." This Sunday, look around in your church and you will see there is a noticeable absence of young people. Then Alexis De Tocqueville wrote that democracy can work in America, because America is a good and moral nation. "America is great because she is good. If America ceases to be good, she will cease to be great." Without our Christian Judeo influence, there would have been no morality in America. Humans are not born moral. Without our Christian Judeo influence, America will destroy itself from within. In "Liberty and Tyranny" Mark Levin wrote, "faith is not a threat to society but rather vital to its survival. It encourages the individual to personally adhere to a dogma that promotes restraint, duty, and moral behavior, which not only benefit the individual but the multitudes and society in general."

Teddy Roosevelt stated, "To educate a man in mind and not in morals is to educate a menace to society." He believed if you were not God-fearing then you might think you were above the laws of man. FDR stated "In the dim distant past they have been Jews, Catholics, and Protestants. What I am more interested in, is whether they were good citizens and believers in God. I hope they were both." Religious faith has been a keystone to the fundamental goodness and morality of America since its founding.

Humans again are not born "good." There are still places on earth where humans are still very primitive. Believe it or not, there are still areas where cannibalism is practiced. Other religions condone killing someone if they disagree with that religion. Some of these same religions teach their children at a very young age that it is alright to kill someone if they believe differently. Children learn their morals from their parents and from society, and in the past in America, Sunday School and or their teachers at school. And if their parents and society are immoral because they have turned away from religion, and their teachers are not allowed to teach manners and morality, then children will grow up without morals or respect for others also. The U.S.A. became the light of the world because it was a more moral nation that treated people fairly and helped people across the world. This generosity and morality came from a religious infrastructure. That infrastructure is deteriorating rapidly. A recent President was caught having extramarital sex, but society basically said, "so what." Athletes do whatever they have to do to win so they will get a bigger contract next year. Ten million isn't enough, they need twenty million. They take performance-enhancing drugs, their coaches put bounties on opposing players to injure them. and take them out of the game. and yet the stadium is still full every Sunday. Recently an NFL quarterback decided to sit down in protest, while the National Anthem was being played. In subsequent weeks, other NFL players have also sat during the anthem, and now high school athletes are copying them. What are they protesting? The lie that police officers are killing young black men because of racism. There is no evidence that this is happening. The last one of these shootings to be reported as police deliberately shooting someone because they were black, involved a black police officer. These athletes with the help of the media, are teaching American children to hate America because of a lie.

Rush Limbaugh reported that a group of seven men affiliated with the NBA, had fathered 55 children with 8 different women and none of these involved marriage, but they play for our favorite team, so we say so what. A few years ago, a boxing champion bit the ear off another fighter. He was also convicted of rape. Yet that same now ex-champion is now a celebrity again and even starred in a Broadway show. Rap artists lyrics contain violent language and language that demeans women and they become wealthy in the process. A mayor from a major city was convicted of buying narcotics and soliciting a prostitute, yet when he was released from jail he was re-elected. Parents punch and abuse referees at pee wee football games because they don't agree with a call. This is telling our children that right and wrong doesn't matter anymore. Religion doesn't matter anymore. Morality doesn't matter anymore. All that matters is winning the game. All that matters it seems, is what you can get away with. Conservatives hate how the network television stations tell half-truths and help fill people with anger with biased information. Yet they still watch their shows and football games and therefore support them. The politicians, (both sides) go to Washington and become wealthy while Americans struggle, yet they keep getting re-elected.

ocrat.

 Divided they stand is working really well, and because the Republicans are not united this plan is even easier to implement. There are some conservatives who really want to restore America to a constitutional government where the people are in charge, but there are also Republicans who want to keep getting elected, so they play the game and sometimes fight the conservatives more than they fight the left. America is no longer indivisible. From the New Testament Mark 3:25, "And if a house be divided against itself, that house cannot stand".

Solutions

Why?

Someone asked me what was I trying to accomplish by writing this book. We live in a world where immediate gratification spurs our decisions. Whatever feels good or sounds good or looks good right now, is in most cases, what motivates people to act or feel a certain way. Young people especially think in the moment. If by telling the truth, telling the facts, and by pulling back the curtain, as they say, opens one person's eyes or one person's heart and helps them have a better life because of those truths, then I have accomplished what I set out to do. If this information gets a young person who may be is at a crossroads in their life, to look at their future and what they might want the rest of their life to look like, and gets them to make some better decisions that will ultimately allow them to have a better life, then I have accomplished what I wanted. If my words help someone to be motivated to get out of the areas where gunshots each night are just accepted part of life, then I have accomplished what I started. If my words get Americans to take control of this country back from corrupt politicians, then I have accomplished what I started. If I can just get people to question why someone is saying something or doing something, i.e., take some responsibility to find out the truth, then I have accomplished what I started. See, it's a good thing to help someone improve their life if you can. As parents, it's our job to improve our children's lives and help them reach their goals to be independent, happy, healthy adults. We do that by educating them, by teaching them what is right and wrong, and by teaching them skills they will need in life. But too many parents are leaving that duty to the media, television, cell phones,

Twitter and Facebook, the politicians, and celebrities. If this information helps a parent put their child on the right path to have a better life, I have accomplished what I wanted. And by opening some eyes and hearts, it helps America to be the great country that has been and can be again the model for the rest of the world, then I have accomplished what I set out to do. Look at the violence and the rioting in Europe. The world is on the fringe of being in a state of great chaos. America is the best place where someone can improve their situation in their life and reach whatever goals they have in their life, but that's no accident. Our system was set up by some men who weren't perfect in their own behavior sometimes. But these men wanted to build a near perfect system that would be different from any other country or nation. They wanted to establish a system that for the first time would be a system that was controlled by the people instead of the government or any one person. For 200 years this system has worked, not perfectly, but it has been by far the best system on Earth. It has been a system that millions have risked their lives to become part of. America has been the moral model, the economic model, and the freedom model for the world, especially since World War II. Recently, that influence has begun to erode, and without that influence, less than desirable factions are filling the void. It's not too late to turn around, but Americans first have to acknowledge what is happening before we can change what is happening. Ronald Reagan said, "If we lose freedom here, there's no place to escape to. This is the last stand on Earth."

Barack Obama was elected President in 2008 and promptly started as he said, fundamentally changing America. However, a quote by Vaclav Claus, former premier of the Czech Republic, really shines a light on the real problem. "The danger to

America is not Barack Obama, but a citizenry capable of entrusting a man like him to the presidency. It will be far easier to limit and undo the follies of an Obama Presidency than to restore the necessary common sense and good judgment to a depraved electorate willing to have such a man for their President. The problem is much deeper and far more serious than Mr. Obama, who is a mere symptom of what ails America. Blaming the prince of the fools should not blind anyone to the vast confederacy of fools who made him their prince. The republic can survive a Barack Obama, who is, after all, merely a fool. It is less likely to survive a multitude of fools such as those who made him their President."

What did President Obama mean when he said he wanted to fundamentally change America? Is it that America is 85% Christian and Jewish believers? Is it that Americans love our liberty? We need to become more involved and let all the politicians know, this is our country. America was built on Christian/ Judeo principals, and we like it that way. The great majority of Americans believe in God and liberty, and we shouldn't feel like we should apologize for that. We need to elect politicians who agree with our beliefs and vote them out when they don't deliver what they promised. We don't want America fundamentally changed. In Mark Levin's book, "Liberty Amendments" he shows a process authorized by our Constitution where the states can call for state conventions to write amendments that would limit the power of the president and the Supreme Court, without going through Congress. This process would require 2/3 of the states to agree to the process, and once amendments were proposed, they would require 34 states to approve before implementing. The Presidency has become too powerful. The Presidency is not a monarch or a dictator. This amendment process could change the possibility of overreaching power that several presidents have taken advantage of. Because of presidential control, the Supreme Court has become too powerful, and they are going above the scope of what they were designed to do. The Supreme Court was designed to interpret how the Constitution applies to certain circumstances. It is not their job to make laws or write words into our laws that weren't there. This amendment process would make the people more powerful than the Supreme Court and make it possible for the people to overrule the court if the voting majority of Americans disagree with their decisions. This process could change that over reaching power whether it's the Presidency, the Supreme Court, or the legislative branch. Power needs to be sent back to the states and the people where it was supposed to be in the first place. Other ideas that I believe will help are term limits on legislatures. We need to elect people that truly want to serve the American people instead of becoming wealthy full-time politicians. It's time to take America back. The ideas and values that made America great are the same ideas and values that can turn America around before it's too late. Believing in God, believing in right and wrong, believing in treating other people right, believing in America and that dreams and hard work can get you anywhere you want to go, these are the ideas and values that will fix the problems we have. Reality, risk, and responsibility are the keys. Seeing the reality of what is going on in our country. Realizing why and how these politicians and media are manipulating the people of America. Taking responsibility and the associated risk to make your life what it should be. Don't like where you are living? Get out! Your job doesn't support your family? Change jobs! There's an old saying, "Working hard and living right creates more luck than 1,000 horseshoes." Working hard and living right is really a simple idea, but it will fix most of the issues we have in this country. Working hard to get through school. Working hard to be a good parent. Working hard at your job or business. Living right as a good neighbor. Living right to be a good example to your children. Treating people with respect. Being honest even when no one is looking.

Turn around. We must turn back to what made America a great country in the first place. Earlier I quoted Alexis De Tocqueville when he said America is a good country. John Adams also commented about the need for morality when he stated, "Our Constitution was made only for a moral and religious people. It is wholly inadequate to the government of any other." Whether you are a Catholic, Baptist, Mormon, Jewish, or whatever faith, we believe in right and wrong. We believe in being good. We believe in God. Patrick Henry stated, "The great pillars of all government and of social life, are virtue, morality, and religion. This is the armor, my friend, and this alone, that renders us invincible" Parents, it's not too late. Grab your children by the arm and tell them, "turn around, we are going this way," We are turning back to God. We are turning back to right and wrong. We are turning back to working hard and trying your best and taking responsibility and making the right choices. We are going to play ball and go fishing and climb trees and wash the car and go camping and hiking or maybe ride a horse, instead of watching hours and hours of television. We need to take our children and volunteer to feed people at the Salvation Army or help build homes with Habitat for Humanity. We need to teach our children about respect and honor and about being honest when no one is looking. Frederick Douglas once stated, "It is easier to build strong children than to repair broken men." Our future lies with our young people. We need people like T.D. Jakes and Dr. Ben Carson and Michael Jordon and Chris Rock to speak to the black community and tell them, "turn around, we are going this way." We need to realize some of the organizations that are race-baiting organizations are not helping minorities. Instead turn to organizations that are helping to educate young people and help them find jobs. Organizations like the Urban League are nonpartisan and they help people instead of inflaming problems. We need Kid Rock, and Ashton Krutcher to speak to the young white people and tell them, "turn around, we are going this way." We need the old white guys, the old black guys, the old latino guys, etc., to grab each other by the arm and tell them, "turn around, we are going this way." This way means treating each other with respect. This way means earning that respect. This way means giving someone a hand up when they need it. Not a hand out. We need the Pope to speak to the latino community and tell them, "turn around, we are going this way." We need the NFL, the NBA, and celebrities in Hollywood to speak to the young people and tell them, "turn around, we are going this way." Athletes used to be role models. We need athletes to think about the young people who idolize them. We need them to set good examples. Whether your neighbor is white or black or Asian or whatever, grab them by the arm and tell them, "turn around, we are going this way." We are going to be good neighbors regardless of the color of our skin. Churches, quit telling the young people what they are doing wrong. You are losing them. Tell them what the right direction is in a positive way and why following God's laws will make their lives better. Teachers, leave politics to the politicians. Turn around and grab your students by the arm and tell them, "turn around, we are going this way." This way, toward right and wrong. This way, treating your parents and other people with respect. Coaches, grab those athletes and parents and tell them, "turn around, we are going this way." This way means playing hard but with sportsmanship. This way means not cheating to win. If you are a CEO, tell your managers and employees, "turn around, we are going this way." This way means treating your employees right and with respect. Richard Branson said the customer isn't the most important person, the employees are. Treat your employees right, and they will treat your customers right.

Turn around, we are going this way. This way means not letting any television station or celebrity tell you how or what to think. Think for yourself. Don't let politicians or celebrities or anyone manipulate the way you think and act. Think about your choices and understand there are consequences for those choices. There are always consequences. If you drop out of school, there are consequences. If you break the law, there are consequences. If you have sex when you are 15, there are consequences. If you don't show up for work, there are consequences. Our politicians need to understand consequences. This means electing people into office who are honest and show character and are truly trying to do what is right, not what will get them reelected. Ask why are they running for this office. The media needs to understand consequences. If you turn the channel they lose money. Turn around, we are going this way. This way means being a good example for your children and being a good neighbor. This way means believing in America.

Local control. If Podunk Texas wants to teach cursive writing, creationism, but not sex education, then it should be up to that community to decide. There is a premise that all schools in all states should be teaching the same thing, that It's not fair to the child if one state doesn't have the same standards as another. Is it fair to impose one area of the countries beliefs on another? With freedom and liberty, there is also responsibility. Parents have relinquished their responsibility to the government to raise their child. Local school boards need to make sure their curriculum will give their students the tools they will need to achieve whatever level of success they are willing to work for. Dr. Benjamin Carson, one of the top neurosurgeons in the country, spoke about how his mother insisted that her two boys read a book every week and then write her a book report, even though she couldn't read the report. That's called parenting. Too often parents today are allowing the internet, television, and video games to shape their children's thoughts and behavior. There are very few consequences for bad behavior any more. Misconduct at school means that you just get sent to an alternative classroom area, that is unless you point your finger at someone like it's a gun, and then you get suspended. So parents need to do more parenting, i.e. read a book to your kids, help them with their homework, and sit down and have dinner together, without their cell phones. Parents need to teach their children social skills, i.e. respect and manners. Parents need to say no sometimes. No, you can't watch that sexually explicit television show, no you can't play that video game that shows someone's head being blown off. No, it's not alright to cheat so you can win a baseball game, no it's not alright to curse at your teacher, no you can't stay up till all hours, no you can't eat cheeseburgers every day, and no its not alright to have sex before you get married just because lots of other kids are. The solutions to all our issues in this wonderful country all lie within us. It's called taking responsibility. As parents, and leaders, and citizens, we must take back control of our country. Our government was set up to serve the people not to control the people. This country of ours, yes ours, not the governments, is like a big ship. It is necessary to get this ship pointed in the right direction again. Because it is a big ship and currently has a lot of momentum in the wrong direction, it will not be easy, and it won't turn quickly. We can turn it around, however, and we must turn it around, or we will lose America. America is the country that people risk their life to come to. It is a place where a young man born in poverty can become a neurosurgeon or a young man, regardless of his skin color, can become the President of the United States. Ronald Reagan called America, a shining city on a hill. That's what it was and can be again. It's up to the people to change this direction. We will destroy our country from within if we don't turn back to the Christian Judeo influence that was the foundation of our morality. We will lose our country if we don't take control back to the people. If the America we have known fails, so will the rest of the world.

Abraham Lincoln summed it up very well when he said, "You cannot bring about prosperity by discouraging thrift. You cannot strengthen the weak by weakening the strong. You cannot help the wage earner by pulling down the wage payer. You cannot further the brotherhood of man by encouraging class hatred. You cannot help the poor by destroying the rich. You cannot keep out of trouble by spending more than you earn. You cannot build character and courage by taking away a man's initiative and independence. You cannot help men permanently by doing for them what they could and should do for themselves."

One benefit of the internet is that things are verifiable as long as you also verify the source. Quit blindly listening to politicians and the media. Quit allowing these people to tell you what to think, what is right and wrong, how to raise your children, or what you should believe. Start thinking for yourself. Question all that you hear or read. Ask yourself, why is this person or group saying this.

What made America great, can be again. E Pluribus Unum. Out of many, one.

Tell the manipulators you will be their puppet no more!